BRIGHT NOTES

THE MAJOR WORKS BY EDGAR ALLAN POE

Intelligent Education

Nashville, Tennessee

BRIGHT NOTES: The Major Works

www.BrightNotes.com

No part of this publication may be used or reproduced in any manner whatsoever without written permission, except in the case of brief quotations in critical articles and reviews. For permissions, contact Influence Publishers http://www.influencepublishers.com.

ISBN: 978-1-645424-14-7 (Paperback)
ISBN: 978-1-645424-15-4 (eBook)

Published in accordance with the U.S. Copyright Office Orphan Works and Mass Digitization report of the register of copyrights, June 2015.

Originally published by Monarch Press.
David Madison Rogers, 1965
2020 Edition published by Influence Publishers.

Interior design by Lapiz Digital Services. Cover Design by Thinkpen Designs.

Printed in the United States of America.

Library of Congress Cataloging-in-Publication Data forthcoming.
Names: Intelligent Education
Title: BRIGHT NOTES: The Major Works
Subject: STU004000 STUDY AIDS / Book Notes

CONTENTS

1)	Introduction to Edgar Allen Poe	1
2)	Textual Analysis	11
	The Poems: Introduction	11
	Fairy-Land	16
	Romance	18
	The City in the Sea	20
	Israfel	22
	A Paean	24
	To Helen	26
	MS. Found in a Bottle	28
	To One in Paradise	35
	The Narrative of Arthur Gordon Pym	38
	Ligeia	46
	The Haunted Palace	52
	William Wilson	54
	The Fall of the House of Usher	60
	The Conqueror Worm	68
	The Murders in the Rue Morgue	70
	Dream-Land	77
	The Masque of the Red Death	79
	The Raven	85
	The Pit and the Pendulum	88

	The Mystery of Marie Roget	94
	The Black Cat	101
	The Premature Burial	107
	The Purloined Letter	113
	The Facts in the Case of M. Valdemar	120
	The Cask of Amontillado	124
	Ulalume	130
	Eldorado	133
	The Bells	135
	Annabel Lee	138
3)	Conclusion	141
4)	Bibliography	144

EDGAR ALLEN POE

INTRODUCTION

EARLY LIFE

Edgar Allan Poe was born in Boston on January 19, 1809. The son of wandering actors, Poe was destined to lead the most tragic life of any major American writer. Misery and bad luck haunted the family. His mother, Elizabeth Arnold Poe, had been a widow at eighteen, and two years after his birth she died of tuberculosis in Richmond at the age of twenty-five. Poe's paternal grandfather had been a wealthy man, but his father, David Poe, had broken with his family to become an actor, and his son was left with nothing. When his mother died, Edgar was adopted by John Allan, a Richmond tobacco merchant, at the urging of his wife. Frances Allan was devoted to him, and in his childhood he enjoyed a measure of security which was never to be his again after he left home. He was raised to be a gentleman and took for granted advantages he was soon to be deprived of. He was well liked as a boy, both by his teachers and his friends, and was a leader in the sports of childhood, particularly swimming at which he excelled. In 1815 John Allan took his family to England in the hope of furthering his business. During the next five years Edgar attended various schools, the most important of which was the Manor House School at Stoke Newington. The gothic atmosphere of this school provided him with many details he was later to make use of in fiction. According to one Master he was an amiable boy and a good scholar.

AT THE UNIVERSITY OF VIRGINIA

In the spring of 1826 Poe entered the University of Virginia, which was then only in the second year of its existence. The atmosphere was not particularly conducive to study. Many of the students brought their horses, dogs, and personal slaves with them. Gambling, drinking, fights, and duels were common, and revelry was hard to avoid. Like many freshmen in every age, Poe was confused and homesick. He learned to play cards for money, and soon he was in debt. Allan, true to his Scotch forebears, had provided his stepson with little cash, and Poe soon owed money to merchants who had given him credit on the strength of his guardian's name. It should be emphasized that Poe was not considered a dashing or gallant young man at the University, nor did he move in really fashionable circles. His debts were not unusual for a young man in his circumstances, and today we would be more likely to call them unpaid bills than debts. It was at this juncture of events that Poe discovered he could not depend upon Allan for financial support. The foster-father refused to pay his debts and Poe had to withdraw from the University. Raised to be a gentleman and trained in the social manners of the pre-war south, at the age of eighteen Poe was abandoned with his education incomplete by a man who refused to see through to its conclusion the responsibility he assumed when he adopted the young Edgar. Poe continued to hope that his foster-father would have a change of heart, but he never did, and when he died, his several illegitimate children were amply provided for, but no mention of Edgar Allan Poe was made in his will.

ENLISTS IN THE ARMY

In May of 1827 Poe enlisted in the army, and in the summer of that year he published his first book, *Tamerlane and Other Poems*. He needed status and economic security, and thought that if he succeeded in his new venture he could make his peace with Allan. In December of 1829 he published his second book, *Al Aaraaf, Tamerlane and Minor Poems*. In June of 1830, a few months after the death of Mrs. Allan, Poe was accepted at West Point. He was respected by both his superiors and his fellow-cadets. When it became apparent, however, that nothing he could do would restore him in Allan's eyes, he wanted to get out of the army. Allan refused to cooperate and Poe deliberately neglected his duties so he would be court-martialed, which he was in January, 1831.

POVERTY AND HIS DRINKING

From 1831 to 1835 Poe lived in poverty in Baltimore. During these years he established the pattern of miserable diet and occasional drinking that eventually brought him to an early grave. In popular tradition Poe is thought of as a great drunkard, but the truth is more complicated than such a statement would suggest. He was brought up in a society that revolved around social drinking, but liquor had a terrible effect on him. He despised debauchery in any form, and yet he did drink. He drank occasionally because it was the habit of the time and because it was a form of charity he could accept without feeling beholden.

And, of course, as his position in life became more and more miserable, he drank as an escape from reality. When he did drink his hypersensitive personality was badly affected.

FIRST LITERARY SUCCESS

In October of 1833 he won a contest sponsored by the *Baltimore Saturday Visiter*, for the story "MS. Found in a Bottle." Through the influence of one of the judges he was employed as an editor of the *Southern Literary Messenger* from July of 1835 to January of 1837. For him it was the first of many editorial positions. Poe brought new life to the literary magazines of America. He despised sentimental sham and was the first really great reviewer in American periodical literature. Often his editorials were original essays on literary criticism. While he was editor he raised the circulation of the magazine from 500 to 3500, but during that time received no more than the $10 a week for which he was originally contracted. Throughout his career he performed enormous editorial labors for ridiculously small salaries.

MARRIAGE

In 1835 he married his cousin, Virginia Clemm, who was at that time thirteen years old. He was twenty-seven. The disparity in their ages strikes the modern reader as absurd, but in the pre-war South it was common for girls to marry when they were very young, a practice that was more often than not the rule in Europe at that time. Modern biographers have attempted to prove that because he married a girl so much younger than himself, his marriage was one in name only. Such a conclusion is absurd. Poe was very much in love with his wife, and at least one observer noted that Virginia kissed him so passionately in public that he found it embarrassing. This does not suggest a passionless, brother-sister relationship. Mrs. Clemm, his aunt, continued to live with them, an arrangement that has provided biographers with much material for speculation. However, the reasons for her continuing to live with them are clear. Poe himself encouraged it. He always felt the need to be mothered, and her presence was a consolation to him. The girl was very young and the mother had nothing else in the world to do. Under such circumstances the arrangement was perfectly natural. Virginia had a harp and a pianoforte, and sang. Mrs. Clemm managed the household. Poe wrote editorials and stories and dreamed of opening his own magazine.

MOVES NORTH

After leaving the *Messenger*, Poe went first to New York, and then to Philadelphia. In July of 1838 Harpers published *The Narrative of Arthur Gordon Pym*, and in December 1839 he published his first collection of stories, *Tales of the Grotesque and Arabesque*. From 1839 to 1842 he worked as an editor for Burton's *Gentleman's Magazine* and *Graham's Magazine*. These were active years for Poe. His controversial reviews stirred interest in literary matters. He wrote features on cryptography, autography, and other subjects which attracted new readers. He was the first editor to acknowledge Hawthorne's genius, and he lauded Tennyson and Mrs. Browning. He detested Longfellow's didacticism and railed against the moralistic tone of literature in New England.

MEETS RUFUS GRISWOLD

In the spring of 1841 Poe met Rufus Griswold (1815-1857), an ambitious editor and anthologist. Griswold was collecting poems for his forthcoming *Poets and Poetry of America*. Poe gave him several poems and influenced several of his friends to contribute. Poe reviewed the book in the Saturday Museum, and implied that Griswold's literary judgment was questionable. From that day Griswold harbored a hatred of Poe that he was too cowardly to express until Poe was dead. In the spring of 1842 Virginia was ill. Years of poor diet and health had resulted in tuberculosis, and for the next four years she suffered terribly until her death in 1847. Poe neglected his duties to help care for his wife, and in May of 1842 Graham brought in Griswold as a substitute, although he had no intention of firing Poe. Appearing suddenly one day, Poe found Griswold in his chair, and in a fit of wounded pride he resigned. He remained on good terms with Griswold, however, never suspecting that the latter harbored a deep hatred for him based on jealousy and wounded pride.

PUBLISHES "THE RAVEN"

In 1843 "The Gold Bug" won a prize from the Dollar Newspaper, and in January of 1845 "The Raven" was published in the *New York Evening Mirror*. Overnight he became famous. "The Gold Bug" had been recently translated into French, and in a year two translations of "The Murders in the Rue Morgue" caused a law suit between two French newspapers. Elizabeth Barrett thought there was "an uncommon force and effect" in "The Raven." Dante Gabriel Rossetti (1828-1882), an English poet of Browning's generation, imitated "The Raven" in his "The Blessed Damozel." Fame, however, did not bring wealth to Poe. The $10 he received for the poem did not go far toward alleviating the wretched condition of his family. In February 1845 Poe began to work for the *Broadway Journal*. Charles F. Briggs, a co-editor of the magazine, came to respect him, in spite of the "abominable lies" he claimed that Griswold had told him about Poe.

DEATH OF HIS WIFE

Virginia Poe was dying and her husband suffered terrible agonies watching her waste away. On January 4, 1848, he wrote to George Eveleth, describing what he experienced:

> Her life was despaired of. I took leave of her forever and underwent all the agonies of her death. She recovered partially and again I hoped. At the end of a year the vessel broke again - I went through precisely the same scene. Again in about a year afterward. The again-again-again and once again at varying intervals. Each time I felt all the agonies of her death- and at each accession of the disorder I loved her more dearly and clung to her life with more desperate pertinacity. But I am constitutionally sensitive-nervous in a very unusual degree. I became insane, with long intervals of horrible sanity. During these fits of absolute unconsciousness I drank, God only knows how often or how much. As a matter of course, my enemies referred the insanity to the drink rather than the drink to the insanity.

She died on January 30, 1847, in Fordham, New York. The Fordham house has been preserved as a museum and stands today as a reminder of nineteenth-century literary America amid the buzzing activity of the Bronx.

RELIGIOUS PHILOSOPHY

Poe lived a little more than two years after the death of his wife and they were the most miserable years of his life. For weeks after Virginia's death he would wander off to her tomb and be found there weeping hysterically. In the spring of the year, as he recovered from the shock of her death, he began to work on *Eureka*, a treatise of some forty thousand words in which he summed up his final attitude toward man and the universe. He discussed the creation and nature of the universe, and its destiny to return to the prime source of being at the end of time. He discarded the method of logic for intuition, but the work was laced with references to Newton, Kepler, Laplace and Humboldt. In a sense the book was an attempt to work out a philosophy of death, a philosophy that would explain the soul's unification, upon death, with the larger spirit that Poe was convinced existed behind the appearances of the universe. One of the rumors that was circulated by his enemies after his death was that he was an atheist. Nothing could be further from the truth. He despised, however, the conventional pictures of heaven and hell, and was groping for a more precise way to discuss the relationship between man and the infinite. He was no more an atheist than Coleridge (1772-1834), English poet and essayist, from whose *Biographia Literaria* he got some of his ideas.

ATTEMPTS SUICIDE

In June of 1848 *Eureka* was published as a book. The next month Poe delivered a lecture in Boston. In a fit of depression he obtained two ounces of laudanum and tried to commit suicide. He did not die, however, but merely made himself sick. He had become acquainted with a poetess, a Mrs. Sarah Whitman, who sent him a valentine with some verses enclosed. As the year progressed he convinced himself that he was in love with her. She shared some of his ideas about religion and was interested in spiritualism. They became engaged late in 1848 but the opposition of Mrs. Whitman's mother wrecked his plans. The family was well off and the mother felt that he was after her daughter's money.

LAST DAYS

In July of 1849 Poe returned to Richmond. He wrote to Mrs. Clemm: "If possible, oh Come? My clothes are so horrible, and I am so ill." Friends arranged for him to give a lecture on "The Poetic Principle" on August 17th at the Exchange Hotel. He lost the manuscript but the lecture was successful anyway. He received invitations to recite "The Raven." He had few decent clothes, however, and seldom accepted such invitations, which were often prompted more by curiosity than genuine interest. He met a woman he had once been engaged to in his youth, Sarah Elmira Royster, now a wealthy widow, and he began to court her again. In the abortive romances of his last years, Poe was desperately attempting to fill the gap in his life that had been left by Virginia's death.

HIS DEATH

In September Poe planned a trip to Baltimore and on the 26th he visited Sarah to say goodbye. He complained of not feeling well, and she said that he left in a high fever. She advised him to see a doctor and he went to a Dr. Carter's office, but the man was not home and he left in a muddled state with the doctor's cane instead of his walking stick. Early the next morning he boarded the steamer for Baltimore. On the morning of September 28th he showed up at the home of Dr. Nathan C. Brooks in Baltimore, noticeably intoxicated. The doctor was not home and he left. For five days he vanished completely. On the third of October, election day in Baltimore, a Mr. Walker, compositor on the *Baltimore Sun*, found him lying in the rain outside Ryan's Public House in which was located the Fourth Ward Polls. He was taken to the Washington College Hospital in a coma. He spoke to imaginary objects on the walls. Hoping to revive his will to live, the doctor told him that in a few days he might be back with his friends. He replied violently that when he thought of his own degradation he was ready to sink into the earth, and that the best thing a friend could do for him would be to blow out his brains with a pistol. He remained delirious. He had been admitted to the hospital on Wednesday. After three and a half days of suffering, at 5 AM on Sunday, the 7th of October, he called out "Lord help my poor soul," and died.

GRISWOLD MALIGNS HIS CHARACTER

Griswold wrote a funeral notice for the *New York Evening Tribune* in which he implied that Poe had drunk himself to death. Three years later, still not feeling himself revenged, Griswold implied that Poe had "criminal relations" with Mrs. Clemm. Other enemies followed suit and soon there was a popular tradition to the effect that Poe was an atheist, a madman, a perpetual drunk, and the very incarnation of evil. In one of the great ironies of American literary history, Griswold became Poe's literary executor and falsified the records to make it appear that his judgment of Poe's character was correct. Mrs. Whitman defended him in her *Edgar Poe and His Critics*, which appeared in 1860 and still has much to offer to the serious student of Poe. The problem of separating fact from fiction and presenting a balanced picture of Poe as a man and a writer has only recently been attacked. It is now recognized, however, in spite of his detractors, that Poe was one of the great writers of America's golden age.

THE POEMS: INTRODUCTION

TEXTUAL ANALYSIS

BASIC PROPOSITIONS OF HIS AESTHETIC THEORY

The foundation of Poe's attitude toward poetry can be stated in the form of a few simple propositions. In literature or any art pleasure is superior to truth and morality. This pleasure comes through glimpses of supernal beauty. We can only experience this ideal beauty in periods of short duration. Poetry in particular must be condensed so it can be appreciated as a whole within a short period of time. Art must be concentrated by emphasis on unity which is governed by necessity. The primary value of poetry is an indefinite elevation of the soul through beauty.

THE GRADES OF BEAUTY

Poe recognized and was affected by three grades of beauty. On the lowest level is the beauty of material objects. The second plane is that of noble thoughts and actions, characteristically thoughts or actions of self sacrifice. The third and most important level is that of beauty of sentiment. In "The Philosophy of Composition" he wrote:

That pleasure which is at once the most intense, the most elevating, and the most pure, is, I believe, found in the contemplation of the beautiful. When indeed, men speak of beauty, they mean, precisely, not a quality, as is supposed, but an effect - they refer, in short, just to that intense and pure elevation of soul -not of intellect, or of heart, upon which I have commented, and which is experienced in consequence of contemplating the beautiful.

All three of these levels of beauty are qualified by the idea of the bizarre in the beautiful.

STRANGENESS AND BEAUTY

Running throughout the English and American romantic periods is the assumption that strangeness adds to or heightens beauty. Poe thought physical landscapes most beautiful when they suggest the bizarre. It was in his heroines, however, that he most emphasized strangeness in beauty. Lady Madeline Usher and Ligeia both have a strangeness in the proportion of their faces that mars the perfection of classic beauty, but renders them more beautiful in Poe's eyes. Poe even insisted that deformity and horror have their place in the beautiful. He wrote in "Fifty Suggestions": "An artist is only an artist by dint of his exquisite sense of Beauty - a sense affording him rapturous enjoyment, but at the same time implying, or involving, an equally exquisite sense of Deformity or disproportion."

UNITY AND PROPORTION

A principle that Poe states with great insistence is that the work of art must communicate a totality of effect. A long poem is a contradiction in terms because if a literary work takes more than one sitting to read everything like totality is destroyed. The essence of totality is proportion. Without proportion there could be no satisfactory unity. In "The Rationale of Verse" he wrote: "Verse originates in the human enjoyment of equality, fitness. Its idea embraces those of similarity, proportion, identity, repetition and adaptation." For Poe, poetry must be formal. **Free verse** is an impossibility.

PROPORTION AND "THE REFRAIN"

One of the chief devices in the creation of proportion in poetry is the use of a **refrain**. The refrain depends for its impression upon the force of monotone both in sound and thought. The pleasure comes from the sense of identity or repetition. Poe used this technique to good effect in "The Raven" and "Ulalume."

MELODY AND RHYTHM IN POETRY

Another device available to the poet is the sheer music of word combinations. Poe thought music to be the highest of the arts. Poetry is only a slightly lower art than music and must make use of the techniques of music. Poetry must have a recognizable rhythm. It does not have to be familiar, but it must be consistent. **Stanzas** are arrangements of words in proportional masses based upon rhythm. Poetry is the creation of beauty through rhythm.

POETRY AND FANCY

Fancy, properly speaking, is an attribute of the poet and not the poem. Unless the poet has "fancies" he has no raw material with which to work. Poe tells us that what he means by a "fancy" is more "physical" than "intellectual." A fancy is a coalescing of image and idea in the soul when it is most tranquil and receptive. Poe wrote of "fancies:"

> They rise in the soul (alas, how rarely!) only at its epochs of most intense tranquility - when the bodily and mental health are in perfection - and at those mere points of time when the confines of the waking world blend with those of the world of dreams. I am aware of these fancies only when I am on the brink of sleep, with the consciousness that I am so. I so regard them, through a conviction (which seems a portion of the ecstasy itself) that this ecstasy, in itself, is of character supernal to human nature-is a glimpse of the spirit's outer world . . ."

Here we have a remarkable account of the mental phenomena to which Poe often turned for the raw materials of his poems.

POETRY AND IMAGINATION

Coleridge provided Poe with his core conceptions about the imagination of the poet. Poe read Coleridge's *Biographia Literaria* in detail. According to Coleridge the imagination of the poet is what enables him to unify his fancies in a cohesive work of art. Without imagination the fancies of the poet would remain disorganized and unable to communicate the unity which Poe thought so necessary in art.

POE'S POETRY

The total body of Poe's poetry is small. He wrote most of his poems rather early in his career and had published a book of poetry before he had even begun to write the great bulk of his tales. They are for the most part brief lyrics, extremely personal and emotional. He wrote most of his poems before he had experienced the economic difficulties that made most of his mature life a nightmare. As with Coleridge, a chaotic life and personal unhappiness made it difficult for him to write poetry, and he wrote very little during the latter part of his life.

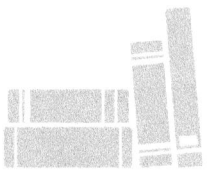

FAIRY-LAND

TEXTUAL ANALYSIS

FORM

"Fairy-Land" is written in iambic **trimeter**. The **rhyme** scheme alternates between **couplets** and an A - B - A - B pattern. There is no exact **rhyme** scheme. The poem is forty-six lines long and is not divided into stanzas.

SUMMARY

> In Fairy-Land there are vales and moods which we cannot see clearly because of the tears that fall everywhere. Huge moons come and go. At exactly midnight an enormous moon buries the land in "A labyrinth of light" and puts all things into a deep sleep. In the morning the moon disappears into the sky. The moonlight dissolves into a shower, however, and earthly butterflies come down from seeking the skies to bring a specimen of that moonlight "Upon their quivering wings."

Comment

"Fairy-Land" is an exercise in pure imagination. There is nothing of the real world in the atmosphere of the poem. As it is described, Fairy-Land is magical, a place where anything can happen and which is lost in drowsy dreams. Here there is no place for reason or the harsh realities of life. The forms of things are only dimly perceived. Their ultimate reality is never known. It is a land of mysteries and Poe is not the least bit interested in solving the mysteries. The chief intention of the poem is to evoke a sense of the indefinite, of the depth and mystery of life which man should accept and delight in.

ESSAY QUESTION AND ANSWER

Question: Discuss Poe's use of humor in the poem.

Answer: In two places Poe makes use of tongue-in-cheek humor in "Fairy-Land." In describing the ascendency of the huge moon at midnight Poe says it is filmier than the rest "(A kind which upon trial/They have found to be the best)." This parenthetical expression has about it a quiet wit that indicates Poe was emotionally detached from the poem. Again, after the moon disappears in the morning, Poe says they will not use it again for the same purpose as before, "Videlicet a tent/Which I think extravagant." Poe's use of the Latin word, which means "namely," is again in the manner of a quiet wit that indicated he was toying with his own poem and not emotionally involved in it. His imagination was quixotic, and often in the middle of an otherwise serious poem he would introduce humorous lines because his enormously quick intelligence saw something amusing in the situation or in the words.

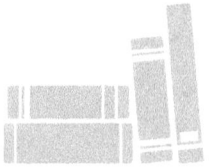

ROMANCE

TEXTUAL ANALYSIS

FORM

"Romance" is a lyric poem in two **stanzas** of ten and eleven lines respectively. There is no exact **rhyme** scheme, although many of the lines are couplets, or alternate according to an A - B - A - B pattern. All the lines are cast in iambic tetrameter.

SUMMARY

Romance is a bird that loves to sing among the green leaves. She taught the poet his earliest words. Of late, though, the poet has been shaken from his dreams by "eternal Condor years" that disturb the world with tumult. When a calmer hour now comes to the poet he would feel it a crime not to allow his heart to lose itself in lyre and rhyme.

Comment

"Romance" is a dramatization of the fate of the poet whose life is increasingly claimed by the affairs of the world when he would prefer to spend his time writing poetry. In the first **stanza** romance is conceived of a luxurious tropical bird nodding and singing on the shore of a "shadowy lake." The **metaphor** is related to the old association between poetry, music, and the singing of birds. The bird has always been used as a symbol for the poet, and the song of the bird stands for poetry. In the poem romance is viewed as the inspirer of poetry.

But the poet is not allowed to indulge himself in his art. His life becomes unquiet like the unquiet sky in the poem. He is forced against his will to pay attention to life. Life claims his attention and he must answer the call. However, in the midst of his involvement in life he still feels the urge to dream and write poetry. The poem is directly autobiographical. If Poe had had a more financially secure position in life it is inevitable that he would have written more poetry. As it worked out he felt impelled to write fiction because he could sell fiction, whereas he could not make money from his poetry. Financial need compelled him to give up what had been in his early years a primary commitment to poetry.

ESSAY QUESTION AND ANSWER

Question: In the second **stanza**, why are the years referred to as "Condor years?" What does the **metaphor** add to the poem?

Answer: The years are referred to as "Condor years" to denote the predatory nature of time. In contrast to the exotic bird of romance in the first stanza, the bird of time is a bird of prey, a fierce and huge bird that is not interested in the world of imagination. The **metaphor** makes graphic the nature of time as it is conceived in the poem. It is from this bird that the poet must steal the treasured but fleeting moments when he can devote himself to poetry.

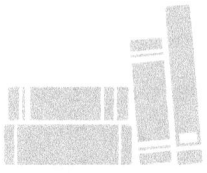

THE CITY IN THE SEA

TEXTUAL ANALYSIS

FORM

"The City in the Sea" is a lyric poem of four sections. The sections are 11, 18, 12, and 12 lines respectively. The poem is written in iambic **tetrameter** couplets, although the poet alters this pattern in several places. The last line of the poem is in iambic trimeter.

SUMMARY

Death has prepared a strange city in the sea. Its towers do not tremble and the water is always quiet. No light from heaven comes down to this city, but rather it is lit by an odd illumination from below. Death presides over the town. The waves begin to stir. The poet says that when the town shall settle among no earthly groans, then Hell shall pay reverence to it from thousands of rising thrones.

Comment

"The City in the Sea" is a period piece handled with great virtuosity. The **theme** of the city of death is not uncommon in the literature of the romantic period. Poe was particularly attracted to the **theme** of death in all its aspects and he explored it at great length in his tales. Poe had a great talent for the sensational and the dramatic, and he indulges both in this poem.

The poem was a favorite of the Pre-Raphaelites in England. They admired Poe's ability to weld sound and sense into a unified verbal structure. The poem is a triumph of brilliant **imagery**. The city is individualized in everything, from the friezes on its walls to "each idol's diamond eye." We are told the friezes intertwine "The viol, the violet, and the vine." Swinburne admired this line for its union of sound and sense. The poem reflects Poe's constant interest in the supernatural and in imaginative constructions that suggest a life beyond what man experiences from day to day.

ESSAY QUESTION AND ANSWER

Question: The poem suggests that man's spiritual life wavers back and forth between two possibilities. What are they and how are they mirrored in the poem?

Answer: In the last **stanza** of the poem Hell is referred to directly. Hell, we are told, shall do reverence to the city of death. The city itself is lit from below, which suggests a link with Hell. At the very beginning of the second section of the poem we are told that the city is untouched by any ray of light from "the holy Heaven." The poem, then, has both **metaphysical** depth and height. That is, in it the life of man is not cut off from the spiritual dimension of life, but rather the life we enjoy on earth is seen as only the very beginning of what will continue after we die.

ISRAFEL

TEXTUAL ANALYSIS

FORM

"Israfel" is a lyric poem of eight stanzas. The stanzas are of 7, 8, 7, 6, 6, 5, 5, and 7 lines respectively. They do not follow any basic pattern of **rhyme** and meter, although they are all closely rhymed, none using more than three rhymes. Most of the lines are in iambic **dimeter** and **trimeter**, although they do not follow an exact pattern.

SUMMARY

In heaven the angel Israfel is the wildest of all singers. The strings of his heart are a lute and when he sings all stop to listen. He despises an "unimpassioned song." The poet says that if he could dwell in heaven with Israfel he might sing better than the angel.

Comment

"Israfel" is a poem about the writing of poetry. It tells us much about what Poe thought of poetry. First of all poetry must be impassioned. A lukewarm poem is no poem at all. Poe thought that perfect poetry was perfect beauty, and hence had a place in the highest reaches of heaven. Poetry, in short, aspires toward the ideal. The ideal toward which poetry aspires can only be imperfectly realized on earth. The poet looks forward to heaven as that state alone in which he will be able to write perfect poetry. "Israfel" makes use of an old tradition that identifies poetry with song. This idea goes back to the wandering bards of the Heroic Age who accompanied themselves with small lyres. Ever since then poetry has been associated with song and with music.

ESSAY QUESTION AND ANSWER

Question: What does the poem reveal of Poe's attitude toward his own work?

Answer: The poem makes it clear that Poe was not satisfied with his own poetry. He writes "this/Is a world of sweets and sours." That is, in this world there can be no perfect poetry. But Poe wanted to write perfect poetry, poetry impassioned beyond the imagination of men. The prevailing tone of the concluding **stanzas** is one of wistful longing. He wants to have an equal chance with Israfel to sing impassioned songs. He is slightly irritated because he labors under the burden of still living in a world of "sweets and sours." He wants the complete sweetness both of life and poetry, and looks forward to the time when he will strike "a bolder note" on his "lyre within the sky."

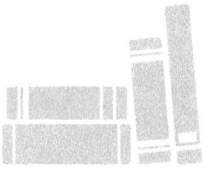

A PAEAN

TEXTUAL ANALYSIS

FORM

"A Paean" is a poem of eleven stanzas. Each stanza has four lines which alternate between iambic **tetrameter** and iambic **trimeter**. The **rhyme** scheme is A - B - A - B.

SUMMARY

> How can the burial rite be read for one who died so lovely and so young? Her friends loved her for her wealth and are secretly pleased that she is dead. Her friends tell the poet he should no longer sing. She has gone above, and the poet is drunk with love for the dead one who was his bride. She has gone to join the "untainted mirth" of heaven. The poet says that since she has gone to heaven he will not sing a requiem, but rather "a Paean of old days."

Comment

One of the commonest **themes** in Poe's work is the death of a beautiful girl. He considered it to be the most melancholy and most proper subject for the poet. In part this was a reflection of the affected melancholy of the romantic period, in part it was a reflection of personal circumstances, the loss of his mother at an early age and the loss of Mrs. Stannard when he was fifteen. In contrast to the pervading melancholy of the time, however, in this poem the poet does not sorrow, but sings his love to heaven.

ESSAY QUESTION AND ANSWER

Question: How does the poem reflect the isolation from society that Poe felt?

Answer: The poem reflects Poe's isolation from society in two ways. The friends of the dead girl appreciated her only for her wealth. The poet loved her for her beauty and for her soul. The poet, in short, is the man who strikes through materialism and seizes upon the beauty and spirituality which alone can feed his soul. The false friends, who stand for society, tell the poet to sing no more. The poet, however, disregards them, and knowing that his love has gone to heaven, sings of the old times they had together, not in sorrow but in joy.

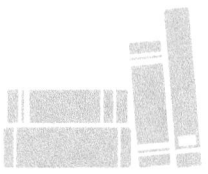

TO HELEN

TEXTUAL ANALYSIS

FORM

"To Helen" is a lyric poem of three stanzas. Each stanza has five lines. The **rhyme** scheme is slightly different in each **stanza** although no more than two **rhymes** are used in each stanza.

SUMMARY

> To the poet, Helen is as beautiful as old ships that carry the weary wanderer home. Her beauty has revealed to him the world of classical Greece and Rome. The realm she comes from is a holy land.

Comment

"To Helen" is one of the most beautiful lyrics in the language. The Helen of the poem was Mrs. Stanard, the mother of one of Poe's close childhood friends Edgar visited her often and to him she represented not only his own mother whom he had lost, but also the very ideal of romantic womanhood. He saw in her all purity and all spirituality. She died when he was fifteen, and Poe was thrown into a deep melancholy by her death. According to John Mackenzie Poe never showed a sign of morbidity except at Mrs. Stanard's death when he appeared "grieving and depressed." Poe wrote the first version of the poem shortly after Mrs. Stanard's death, but he continued to revise it and the poem did not reach its final form until late in his life.

ESSAY QUESTION AND ANSWER

Question: The poem is completely dependent upon classical references. Perhaps the name Helen suggested to Poe all that richness of classical reference with which he had become thoroughly familiar. Poe had been given a classical education and to him such references were completely natural.

Answer: In the first **stanza** Poe compares Helen's beauty to the ships of Nicea, a city near the Sea of Marmara. In the second **stanza** he refers to her "Naiad airs." In Greek and Roman mythology a naiad was a spirit that occupied springs, fountains, rivers, and lakes. Her naiad airs, we are told, have brought the poet home "To the glory that was Greece/ And the grandeur that was Rome." These lines are perhaps the most often quoted of any that Poe wrote. In the last **stanza** he refers to Helen as Psyche, a Greek personification of the soul. Poe makes these references in a natural, unstudied way. They give the poem a depth it would not otherwise have.

MS. FOUND IN A BOTTLE

TEXTUAL ANALYSIS

CHARACTERS

Narrator, a man of wealth and education

The Swede, a superstitious sailor

PLOT ANALYSIS

The narrator sails from the port Batavia, on a voyage to the Archipelago Islands. The vessel is caught in a calm off the coast of Java. One night the narrator notices an odd could on the horizon. The moon is red and the sea unusually transparent. The captain scoffs at the narrator's presentiment of danger, and all go to sleep. Shortly after midnight the ship is struck by high winds and tumultuous waves. All on board perish except the narrator and an old Swede. For five days they are driven south by high winds. On the sixth day they are "enshrouded in pitchy darkness." The Swede gives way to superstitious terror and the narrator is "wrapt in silent wonder." The ship alternately rises and sinks in a still tempestuous sea. In the backwash of a great swell they suddenly perceive above them a huge, black ship which casts "a dull, sullen glare of red light" on the rolling sea. The strange ship smashes down upon them and the narrator is cast by the shock into the rigging of the black ship. The Swede goes down with the wreck.

The men of the odd ship have about them the atmosphere of great antiquity. In awe of them the narrator hides himself in the hold. Their instruments are ancient and they use outdated charts. As the days pass the narrator feels a new sense added to his soul. He is possessed by feelings for which he has no name. The men pass him by without seeing him, wrapped in meditations he does not understand.

The ship itself is a mystery. The bow is "severely simple" and the stern "antiquated." There is about the ship as well as the men "an unaccountable memory of old foreign chronicles and ages long ago." The narrator is unable to identify the material from which the ship has been made. It is unusually porous. The narrator is keeping a diary and decides to put it into a bottle and cast it into the sea.

The captain of the black ship has upon his face "the thrilling evidence" of utter old age. He speaks a language the narrator does not know. The age of the captain excites in the narrator "a sentiment ineffable." About a mile from the ship on either side begin to tower stupendous walls of ice as they continue southward. The narrator believes the ship is being rushed along by an unknown current, and speculates that it may lead to the South Pole itself. The crew crowds onto the deck with expressions of eagerness and hope. The ship plunges suddenly into an immense whirlpool and disappears.

CHARACTER ANALYSIS

Narrator

The narrator is a man of great hereditary wealth and unusual education. He has no longer any feeling either for his family or his country, having been driven from the former by "ill usage," and from the latter by long years of wandering. He tells us that he has always been deficient in imagination, and that he is dedicated to scientific truth. The experience that the narrator undergoes in the story opens up to him realms of life that he had never dreamed of. Dedicated to scientific truth, the extreme old age of the captain awakens in him feelings he is unable to name. We are told he is thrilled by this experience of antiquity. Everything the narrator encounters on the ship defies the one faculty he had before held in veneration-reason. He is made gradually aware of the fact that vast areas of life lie outside the precincts of clear-cut and understandable truth. The apprehension of this new world is, however, associated with danger. Danger, in fact, has been partly responsible for awakening in him the capacity to wonder at the mystery of life and death. As the story proceeds, and his soul is further expanded in the apprehension of mystery, the danger increases until death, the ultimate mystery, stares him in the face as the ship goes down.

The Swede

The Swede is a minor, but important character in the tale. On the sixth day, when the drifting wreck is encompassed by darkness, it is the Swede who is overcome with superstitious terror. His terror is the reaction of the uneducated man to the revelation of worlds beyond his understanding. The Swede only speaks one sentence in the tale. As the black ship comes into view on the crest of the swell above them, he cries out: "See, see!" ... "Almighty God! see! see!" What the Swede sees is not simply the black ship, but a world beyond his own. His own limited view of life is shattered by the appearance of an object that suggests life and experience far beyond what he can understand. The reaction of the Swede is measured against that of the narrator. The narrator is rendered solemn and awestruck. The Swede is terrified.

Comment

"MS. Found in a Bottle," is an important story in Poe's career. In July 1833 it won a contest sponsored by the *Baltimore Saturday Visiter*, and through John Pendleton Kennedy, one of the judges and a novelist and lawyer of note, Poe obtained his first editorial position. He had read a great deal about the sea in travel books and technical treatises on sailing craft, and the facts he had absorbed enabled him to create an atmosphere of **realism** in the tale. What might be called the psychological background of the story revolves around both facts and myths associated with the sea. The storm, the whirlpool, the fascination of unknown areas like the South Pole, stories of unknown ships appearing out of nowhere-all these had been known to the American reading public long before Poe. Such stories are legendary and provide a natural foundation for imaginative fiction. Poe returned to them again in "Descent into the Maelstrom" and *The Narrative of A. Gordon Pym*. The foundation of such stories is both fact and legend.

Poe begins "MS. Found in a Bottle" with an atmosphere of fact and with a main character who is dedicated to fact. We are told that the ship the narrator sails on was built in Bombay of Malabar teak and is carrying a cargo of oil, cocoanuts, ghee and a few cases of opium. These are facts presented as facts and the reader accepts them in the same way that he would accept the facts in a travel book. However, after he has forced the reader's assent to the truth of the experience, the story becomes more and more fantastic. Even the facts themselves, however, suggest the mysterious and unknowable. Bombay and Malabar are words that conjure up for the western reader images of an exotic and distant world. The reader very soon enters such a world in the story.

What is the ultimate point of a story such as this? Is it meant simply to thrill the reader, to entertain him, or is the horror, the fantastic incident simply a means to an end that lies far beyond mere titillation? Poe, like Wordsworth (1770-1850) and the other romantics, was dedicated to the truth of the heart, the world of spiritual reality. He was fascinated by the idea that there lay just beyond the comprehension of men a world of spirit that dwarfs our world of everyday reality, and yet impinges on it everywhere. Very often his tales have to do with the meeting of these two worlds in death and near death, and the circumstances that break down the barriers between the commonplace and transient, the mysterious and eternal. Surely the reader is entertained by "MS. Found in a Bottle." He may even be frightened or horrified by it. Perhaps more likely, he will finish the tale with the feeling that he has been in contact with a mystery, a mystery which is far closer to what is truly real than the drab lives men often lead. That Poe chose the means he did to approach the spiritual world is the result of his own character and the literary and cultural **conventions** of his own day. The mystery is never defined. We are never told exactly what the spiritual world is or what happens there. We do know that it exercises a transforming power on the life of men, that it is greatly exciting, and that it has immense possibilities for good and evil. The tale is meant to make the reader feel as if he had glimpsed some aspect of infinity.

It is clear that in many of the details of his characters' lives Poe projected his own hopes, fears and situations. All his life Poe longed for the security of wealth and family tradition, a security he experienced as a child and from which he was cut off. The narrator is a man of wealthy family. However, he is a man cut off, an outcast, a wanderer in the world. The world of the mysterious opens to him precisely because he has become one apart, one removed from the normal **conventions** and life of humanity. It is clear that Poe used his own practical and psychological situation in the tales. So many of his characters would not have been wanderers had he not been one himself. However, this projection of himself is not the purpose or the point of the tale. Too many biographers and critics have attempted to point out the relationship between Poe's character and the tales, without also pointing out that the tales exist as complete worlds of fiction apart from the character of the author.

ESSAY QUESTIONS AND ANSWERS

Question: From what point of view is the story written? What relationship is there between the point of view and the dramatic effect of the tale?

Answer: The story is told from the point of view known as the first person. Everything in the tale is seen through the eyes of the narrator. Novels are more often told from the omniscient point of view, since the novelist has to be able to explain the motivation of many characters. The short story is particularly well adapted for the uses of the first person point of view. Poe was one of the first masters of the short story, and some scholars think that he did more than any other writer to establish and develop the form of short fiction as something distinct from the novel. Poe felt that the tale should lead to an overwhelming crisis by steps of rigid logic. His intention, then, was to give the reader a dramatic experience. The experiences Poe deals with are often unusual.

To make them more believable Poe uses the technique of the narrator. The narrator is often a man with whom the reader can sympathize, and the reader starts by accepting as believable the character of the narrator, and ends by accepting as believable, for the purposes of the story, the experiences undergone by the narrator. The dramatic effect of Poe's tales often depends upon the reader's being involved in the character of the narrator as well as the action. The one makes the other more believable.

Question: Discuss the conclusion of the tale. What technique does Poe use to make it dramatic?

Answer: Throughout the tale the reader experiences through the words of the narrator all the unusual action. The story is cast in the form of a personal document, a journal which is to be put in a bottle and cast into the sea. Instead of writing the wind was in the poop, and casting the action in the past, Poe writes "the wind is still in our poop," "we are plunging madly within the grasp of the whirlpool." The reader, then, is present at the time the action is unfolding. Although it is not strictly logical, Poe has us experience the act of going down with the ship, through the words of the narrator: "the ship is quivering-oh God! and going down!" The use of the present tense becomes unusually dramatic at the conclusion of the story because of the peculiar circumstances of the conclusion. It is not, perhaps, completely logical to believe that a man would be writing in his journal at such a moment. It is even harder to believe that he would have time to put the manuscript in the bottle as the ship was going down. However, we accept his being able to do so in the same way that we accept the last aria of the dying Mimi in La Boheme, or the ability of the cowboy hero to shoot the gun out of the villain's hand at an incredible distance. They are **conventions** and we accept them as such.

TO ONE IN PARADISE

TEXTUAL ANALYSIS

FORM

"To One in Paradise" is clearly one of the finest poems that Poe ever wrote. It is a lyric poem in four **stanzas** of 6, 7, 7, and 6 lines respectively. The lines are for the most part in iambic **trimeter**, although there are **tetrameter** lines in each **stanza** but the last. Several of the **trimeter** lines have an extra syllable which gives them a lilting quality, and they are contrasted nicely with those that do not. The **rhyme** scheme is not constant, but the basic pattern is A - B - A - B - C - B - C. The **stanzas** are closely rhymed, particularly the last **stanza** which uses only two rhymes.

SUMMARY

The poet addresses his lover in paradise and says that she was everything to him, an isle, a fountain, and a shrine. He hears a voice from the future that urges him on, but his dejected spirit lingers in the past. For him life is over because the one he loved is dead. His days are trances and at night he dreams constantly of his beloved in paradise.

Comment

A close analysis of a poem like "To One in Paradise" demonstrates clearly that neither originality nor power of thought are required for a classic lyric poem. Given a **theme**, a feeling, it is aptness and beauty of expression that make the poem great. The intellectual core of "To One in Paradise" is extremely simple, its execution superb. The first **stanza** utilizes three metaphors, all of which have a symbolic value. The poet says that his love was to him a "green isle," and "A fountain and a shrine." Isle, fountain, and shrine function as symbols of his love and they are all surrounded with happy connotations. Islands from the dawn of time have symbolized edenic innocence and freedom. Fountains have always symbolized the very source of life itself, and the shrine, of course, stands for the height of man's devotion. Poe is able to incorporate all this symbolism into a **stanza** notable for its simplicity and directness.

In the third **stanza** Poe wants to express the effect of lost love. He does this simply and powerfully by again using concrete images. In a double **metaphor** he compares himself to a "thunder-blasted tree" and a "stricken eagle." The last **stanza** is a triumph of melodic language and deserves to be quoted in its entirety

And all my days are trances, And all my nightly dreams Are where thy dark eye glances, And where thy footstep gleams - In what ethereal dances, By what eternal streams.

The English romantic poets can boast of no more beautifully turned stanza.

ESSAY QUESTION AND ANSWER

Question: Discuss Poe's use of dialogue in the poem.

Answer: In two places Poe uses dialogue in the poem, a fact that is remarkable in such a brief poem of sharp lyric intensity. In the second **stanza** a voice from the future cries "On! on!" to the failing poet. Again, in the third **stanza** the sea is conceived of as speaking to the shore: "No more-no more-no more." These two interjected statements give a dramatic quality to an otherwise purely lyric poem. The **stanzas** is which they occur are stanzas of movement, in contrast to the introductory first **stanza** and concluding fourth.

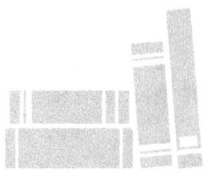

THE NARRATIVE OF ARTHUR GORDON PYM

TEXTUAL ANALYSIS

CHARACTERS

Arthur Gordon Pym, a young adventurer

Augustus Barnard, his friend, son of a sea captain

Dirk Peters, a sailor

PLOT ANALYSIS

Arthur Gordon Pym is the son of a Nantucket trader. At school he meets Augustus Barnard and they become close friends, sharing the same room. One night after a party Augustus wakes Pym up and leads him in a wild midnight escapade in Pym's boat. Pym does not realize that Augustus is intoxicated until the boat is far out to sea. Augustus collapses in the bottom of the boat, and Pym is terrified because he is not an experienced sailor. Their ship is run down by a whaler, but they are both rescued and returned to Nantucket.

Captain Barnard, Augustus' father, is fitting out the Grampus for a whaling voyage upon which Augustus is to accompany him. The boys work out a plan to hide Pym in the hold until the ship is too far out to sea to turn back. Augustus hides Pym in a large box with enough food and water for four days. On the fourth day Pym discovers to his horror that the trap door through which he had entered the hold is barred. Augustus does not come to lead him back, as was planned. He remains in the hold several days more, becoming weak from thirst and starvation. Finally Pym's dog appears unexpectedly at his side bearing a message from Augustus that tells him he must lie low to preserve his life. Pym is sick from fever and hunger when Augustus finally appears. He tells Pym that the crew mutinied a few days after the ship put to sea and that they are both in great danger. One of the mutineers, Dirk Peters, helps the boys get food.

During a storm some of the mutineers are washed overboard. Peters and the boys surprise the remaining mutineers and kill all of them except a sailor named Parker. The ship is pounded to a hulk by heavy seas. Desperate for food, they decide to eat one of their number so that the others may survive, and draw lots to determine who will be eaten. Parker is chosen to be eaten and they live for three days upon his flesh. The survivors are picked up by the Jane Guy of Liverpool, bound for the South Seas.

They stop at an island and discover natives living in a state of complete savagery. Before the landing party can depart, the natives kill all but Pym and Peters by trapping them in an earth slide. Next the savages attack the ship. Pym and Peters watch helplessly from the shore as they overcome the crew. In exploring the ship, however, the natives accidentally set off the ammunition and about a thousand of them are killed in the resulting blast.

Pym and Peters discover ruins on the island that remind Pym of ancient Babylon. They find an unguarded canoe and put to sea in it. The savages chase them unsuccessfully. The canoe enters a strangely warm sea which causes them to become sleepy. A white, ashy substance like that expelled by volcanoes begins to fall all about them. The boat is sucked up into a huge cataract and an enormous human figure, white as snow, rises in front of the boat. The journal of Arthur Gordon Pym ends upon this cryptic note.

CHARACTER ANALYSES

Arthur Gordon Pym

The youthful hero of the tale is above all things an adventurer. It is his impetuous temperament and that of his friend Augustus that keeps the tale moving from **episode** to episode. When the captain of the Jane Guy considers turning back rather than proceeding farther south into the Antarctic, it is Pym who changes his mind, lured by the idea of seeing what no man had ever seen before. Projected into horror after horror by his thirst for adventure, Pym is blessed with a singularly unreflective mind in which the memory of awful events quickly fades away. We are told, for example, that his eating of Parker's flesh soon takes on in his mind the character of a nightmare dimly remembered. The event loses its reality. Pym is young and in Poe's characterization he is unconscious of everything but present reality. Poe's picture of youth is realistic in this respect, although the events in which Pym is engaged are obviously fantastic.

Augustus Barnard

Augustus and Pym are two of a kind. His characterization is not given personality, as such, any more than that of Pym. He is simply a young man in search of adventure, and constitutionally unable to consider consequences or reflect upon the meaning of human experience. For him, to be involved in action is all. At the beginning of the story it is he who propels them into the midnight boat ride that almost results in disaster. Poe himself as a young man enjoyed sheer physical adventure and loved to go off on fishing and swimming expeditions with his friends along the James River. *Pym* was the last tale in which Poe traded heavily upon his childhood experience.

Dirk Peters

The friendly mutineer is important because he is a good example of Poe's maturing ability to picture the exotic and horrible in realistic, believable terms. We are told he is the son of an Indian woman and a fur trader. His arms and legs are bowed, his hands thick and broad, his head bald. The passage that follows, which continues to describe Peters, is a good example of Poe's technique in making real the essentially imaginative:

> The mouth extended nearly from ear to ear; the lips were thin, and seemed, like some other portions of his frame, to be devoid of natural pliancy, so that the ruling expression never varied under the influence of any emotion whatever. This ruling

expression may be conceived when it is considered that the teeth were exceedingly long and protruding, and never even partially covered, in any instance, by the lips.

The portrait is almost scientific in its detail and objectivity, and yet the object of the description is purely imaginative, the creation of the author's mind from certain facts of human physiognomy. Poe admired the realistic technique of Daniel Defoe in *Robinson Crusoe*, which he thought one of the greatest English novels. He extended the use of this technique by applying it to purely imaginary subjects.

Comment

In March of 1836 Mr. Paulding of Harpers wrote to Poe and told him they would be glad to accept a long story for publication. He began at once to work on a longer piece that would satisfy their requirements. He decided to write an adventure story dealing with young men at sea. Such tales were very popular at the time in an age when there were still vast tracts of ocean left unknown. As in "MS. Found in a Bottle," he based the story upon a wide, though secondary knowledge of sailing, geography, and physical phenomena in general. He had read John Clove Symmes' *Symzonia* which had suggested that the earth was hollow with access to the interior through great holes at either pole. This idea suggested to him the conclusion of *Pym*. Most of the details of the story Poe took from Benjamin Morrell's *Narrative of Four Voyages to the South Seas and Pacific*, 1822-1831.

At the time that he was working on *The Narrative of A. Gordon Pym*, Poe was employed by the *Southern Literary Messenger*. He had contributed very little to the November (1836) issue of the magazine and was afraid that he might be dismissed. He offered the first two **episodes** of *Pym* to the editor-in-chief and they were accepted and published in January and February. The entire story was published as a small book by Harpers in 1838, but it was a failure, and even the first edition failed to sell out. *Pym* was offered to the public in the form of an elaborate literary hoax. An introductory note supposedly written by A. G. Pym himself informed the reader that the experiences of the author were true, but that since he himself was but a poor writer he had agreed to have one Mr. Poe of the *Southern Literary Messenger* write up the earlier part of his adventures and publish them as fiction. The public did not accept the adventure as fiction, the note goes on, so that he, Pym, decided at length to publish a full factual account of what actually happened under his own name. Such hoaxes were extremely popular in the early nineteenth century and constituted a kind of literary game. Sometimes the author was a true traveler, but tried to palm off his adventures as fiction. Perhaps more commonly, an author would attempt to convince the public that his fictional adventure had really taken place. The public's part in the game was to guess the truth. The author's part was to entertain the public at the same time he was deceiving it.

The structure of *Pym* is episodic. There is no one single overwhelming **theme** other than that of travel and danger in itself. The various adventures are like beads on a string. The story is achieved by adding episode to **episode**. The cryptic conclusion of the tale, however, suggests that Poe may have had in mind an idea that is not fully explored in the action of the piece. What are we to think of the mysterious white figure that rises in the path of the boat? Is he, like Melville's white whale, meant to symbolize the force, the power behind all the visible phenomena of the universe? The color white is also emphasized in the ashes that fall upon them as they are swept into the cataract. Ashes have always been associated with dissolution and the end of bodily existence. Perhaps Poe simply utilized all the images he could command to suggest the crumbling of earthly existence, without having any particular idea in mind. If this is the case, the enormous white figure is possibly meant to suggest the enormity and power of the world they are about to enter, the world beyond the flesh that so many of Poe's characters attempt to take by storm. The exact meaning of the conclusion will no doubt be a matter of debate among literary critics for some time to come.

ESSAY QUESTIONS AND ANSWERS

Question: Does the structure of *Pym* reflect in any way the manner in which it was composed and the purpose for which it was intended?

Answer: As we have seen, Poe published the first half of the narrative in the form of two installments in the *Southern Literary Messenger*. The first adventure in which the boys are run down by a whaler on their midnight escapade, is complete in itself and can be understood without reference to the rest of the story. The second **episode**, describing Pym's excruciating ordeal in the pitch-black hold of the Grampus, is more closely related to the rest of the tale. The episodic nature of the plot, particularly in the first half of the story, reflects the fact that he designed the early sections for publication in a magazine.

Pym was designed from the beginning to be an extended adventure story in the hope of capturing the rather large audience that such tales could claim in the 1830s. The only continuous **theme** in the story is that of the voyage itself. The idea of the extended voyage relieved Poe from the necessity of conceiving a plot that would develop as the complication of a single action or set of circumstances.

Question: In what way is *The Narrative of A. Gordon Pym* different from all the other tales that Poe wrote?

Answer: *Pym* is the only attempt Poe ever made to compose a story of novel length. All his other stories are short, quite literally short stories, and are centered around a single **climax**. Even *Pym* is more like a series of short stories about the same characters than a true piece of extended fiction. There are many minor climaxes in *Pym*, none really differentiated from the others in terms of dramatic precedence except the final sucking of the boat into the cataract at the end. Poe's need for ready cash and his association with magazines directed his attention to the tale as a form rather than the novel.

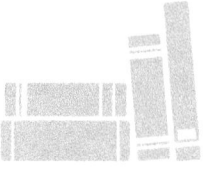

LIGEIA

TEXTUAL ANALYSIS

CHARACTERS

Narrator, Lady Ligeia, Lady Rowena, Trevanion

PLOT ANALYSIS

The narrator speaks of his love for the Lady Ligeia, and of her character. He cannot seem to remember either the name of her family or the place in which he first met her. He is sure, however, of the antiquity of her family. She was tall, slender, and before she died, emaciated. Her face was beautiful, but had some irregularity he cannot identify. Her eyes, lashes and hair were black. When her beauty had passed into his spirit, the narrator felt a sentiment akin to what he feels when contemplating a butterfly or a stream of running water. Her will, thought, and action were intense in the extreme, and although outwardly calm, she was a "prey to the tumultuous vultures of stern passion." Her knowledge was great and included all the classical tongues. In the past she had helped the narrator pursue his esoteric studies. Ligeia became ill but longed for life. As she gradually approached death her desire for life became more and more intense. She was obsessed with the idea that men must die only because of the weakness of their wills. At her death the narrator was plunged into despair.

A wealthy man, he purchases an abbey in England and devotes his time to restoring it. He becomes "a bounden slave in the trammels of opium," and surrounds himself with exotic objects, golden candelabra, and stained glass from Venice. Into the restored abbey he brings a new bride, the Lady Rowena Travanion. She is afraid of him and he comes to detest her.

In the second month of their marriage Lady Rowena is taken ill. She becomes nervous and excitable, and speaks of sounds and motions of which the narrator is unaware. On a night in September the narrator is sitting by the bed of his obviously dying wife. He feels a palpable but invisible object pass close to him. He gives a goblet of wine to Lady Rowena, but before she drinks it several drops of a ruby colored fluid appear in the wine which the ailing woman swallows without hesitation. Her condition immediately takes a turn for the worse and in three days she is dead. During this time the narrator has almost continuous visions and thoughts of the Lady Ligeia.

At about midnight he hears a sob from the shrouded corpse of his wife. The sound is repeated three times with increasing volume. The corpse rises and totters toward him. He runs to her, but at his touch the figure draws back and looses from her head "the ghastly cerements which had contained it." Huge masses of long black hair tumble down the side of the figure. The eyes of the revived corpse open, and the narrator, in a frenzy of excitement, looks into the wild eyes of the Lady Ligeia.

CHARACTER ANALYSES

Narrator

The narrator is a typical romantic hero. He has a passion for absolute knowledge and for his love, the Lady Ligeia. In his quest for absolute knowledge he is like Faust, and in his romantic love he is like Byron. The romantic hero is never content with what he possesses, but is constantly striving to understand or love more than he has in the past. He withdraws from the world so he may more perfectly pursue the objects of his passion. In Poe the desire for absolute knowledge takes the form of a longing to enjoy an eternal life that is not subject to the ravages of time and death. The secret of this eternal life is what his heroes are searching for in their esoteric knowledge. His characters are obsessed with the idea that if they can only discover the proper formula the eternal life will open to them. A natural outcome of this obsession is the frequency with which they attempt to make contact with the supernatural world. Visitations from the dead are common. Attempts to communicate with the dead evidence Poe's fascination for the idea of eternal life beyond the grave. The narrator becomes an opium addict, searching for a way to forget the loss of Ligeia and enter the supernatural world he longs for. The taking of drugs has often been associated with writers of the romantic period, particularly as an escape from the world of everyday reality. Among the English romantics, Coleridge (1772-1834) and de Quincey (1785-1859) were known to be takers of opium. Ironically, as much as the narrator wants to enter the supernatural world, when he comes face to face with his wife who has come back from the dead, he is horrified. In Poe's fiction the breaking down of the barrier between the living and the dead is often desired, but when it is actually accomplished the characters are filled with dread. The narrator's abbey is filled with exotic objects and is reminiscent of the House of Usher. The narrator is a man for whom the ordinary world is too dull to be endured.

Lady Ligeia

Lady Ligeia is the quintessential romantic heroine. Her pale, slightly irregular face was a popular ideal of beauty in the early nineteenth century. Perhaps less popular as a widespread ideal was her highly developed reason and will. They make her an essentially cold character. She is spoken of as having a "marble" hand. Her great passion, besides her love for her husband, is for a life that will not be subject to the ravages of time and disease. Her desire, however, becomes inverted, so that it is the life of this world she wants to enjoy in perpetuity, and it is to this end that she directs her intense will.

Lady Rowena Trevanion

Lady Rowena is completely dismayed by her husband's fascination for the exotic. She does not understand him, and what to him seems laden with super-natural significance is to her only morbid. She is a representative of the normal, the ordinary world the narrator despises so much. He marries her only to forget the Lady Ligeia, but succeeds only in irritating himself, because she is Ligeia's opposite. The difference between the two women is symbolized by their hair. Ligeia has raven-black hair, suggestive of mystery and night, while Rowena has golden hair and despises the mysterious.

ESSAY QUESTIONS AND ANSWERS

Question: Discuss Poe's use of repetition and pause to achieve dramatic effect.

Answer: Poe uses repetition for emphasis in "Ligeia." For example, he writes: "In halls such as these-in a bridal chamber such as this-I passed, with the Lady of Tremaine, the unhallowed hours of the first month of our marriage-passed them with but little disquietude." Poe often repeats not simply a single word, but prepositional phrases and verbs as well. The piling up of similar words and phrases in an intricate verbal network, often involving **alliteration** and **assonance**, serves to emphasize the uniqueness of the narrator's surroundings and to suggest the passage of time. Poe is writing a short story and the demands upon space are great. Through repetition he is able to suggest by rhetorical pace alone the passage of a month's time.

Toward the end of "Ligeia," Poe uses dashes and commas frequently to achieve dramatic suspense. For example, he writes: "I trembled not-I stirred not-for a crowd of unutterable fancies connected with the air, the statue, the demeanor of the figure, rushing hurriedly through my brain, had paralyzed-had chilled me into stone." The last sentence of the story, in particular, is notable for the use of punctuation to achieve dramatic suspense. "'Here then, at least,' I shrieked aloud, 'can I never-can I never be mistaken-these are the full, and the black, and the wild eyes-of my lost love-of the Lady-of the Lady Ligeia'." Although perhaps overdone in places, such a sentence indicates that Poe fully comprehended the use of punctuation to reinforce **theme** in fiction.

Question: A five **stanza** poem, supposedly written by Ligeia, is included in the story. What function does it fulfill?

Answer: The **theme** of the poem is death in its most reprehensible aspect, that of the dissolution of the flesh. The title of the poem in Poe's complete works is "The Conqueror Worm," taken from the last line. In the poem an angelic though weeping throng watch a play, the tragedy "Man." The actors are like puppets and move at the bidding of "vast formless things." The hero of the piece is the worm, symbolic of decay and dissolution. The worm is a "hero" only because it wins in the end. It is against precisely this that the Lady Ligeia is determined to exercise her fierce will. She must escape the common end of all flesh. Somehow she must find a way to avoid the decay of the body. The method she decides upon is simply the summoning of all her powers of will to defy death. She will not die. The poem dramatizes with considerable force the human limitation that Ligeia finds most repulsive.

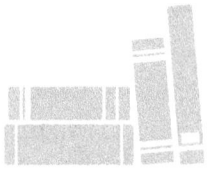

THE HAUNTED PALACE

TEXTUAL ANALYSIS

FORM

"The Haunted Palace" is a stanzaic poem. There are six stanzas in the poem, each consisting of eight lines. The lines alternate between trochaic **tetrameter** and **trimeter** in no exact pattern, and with at least one dimeter line in each **stanza** except the last. Although the stanzas are not arranged in any exact pattern, they appear to be arranged in a pattern, and only a detailed examination will prove they are not.

SUMMARY

A palace once stood in a green valley in the dominion of the monarch Thought. In olden times glorious golden banners floated over its roof. Wanderers in the valley saw Spirits in the castle moving to the music of a lute around the throne of the wise ruler. Things of evil assailed the monarch and now travelers in the valley see "Vast forms, that move fantastically/To a discordant melody." Hideous throngs rush from the castle and laugh, but never smile again.

Comment

In "The Fall of the House of Usher" Poe attributes "The Haunted Palace" to Roderick Usher, although in the story the poem is untitled. The poem, with its **theme** of goodness and virtue overthrown by evil spirits, suits the theme of the tale. The action of the poem is timeless and takes place in the timeless land of Thought. The good and evil of the poem are spiritual good and spiritual evil. The poem reflects Poe's feeling that he was at the mercy of forces beyond his control.

ESSAY QUESTION AND ANSWER

Question: In the last line of the poem we are told that a throng rushes from the palace laughing, but never to smile again. Explain the meaning of the last line.

Answer: Throughout the poem the poet has been describing a tragedy of grotesque implications. Good is overthrown by horrible, nameless "forms." The effect of these forms upon the good spirits is to make them flee, laughing. Their laughter, however, is not healthy. They laugh like maniacs who have lost control of themselves through shock. Hysterical laughter has always been associated with the behavior of lunatics, and Poe makes use of this tradition in the poem. The good spirits do not smile because smiling would be a sign of sanity and health.

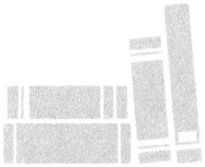

WILLIAM WILSON

TEXTUAL ANALYSIS

CHARACTERS

Narrator, William Wilson

PLOT ANALYSIS

The narrator says he will call himself William Wilson. The implication is that this is an assumed name. He says he is an outcast among men and the detestation of his race. He has committed an unpardonable crime which goes unmentioned. Rather than becoming base by degrees, he says that he lost all virtue in a moment. Like Roderick Usher he is the descendant of a race known for its imaginative and nervous excitability. He recalls his school days in a rambling Elizabethan mansion. The house was irregular and it was easy to lose one's way in it. He recalls how impressive the rector was, ascending his pulpit on Sunday morning. A young scholar arrived with the same name as himself. The narrator was known as a boy of spirit and does not like the newcomer's challenge to his status among their fellows. In character and physical appearance he is like the narrator. He manifests an obvious affection for the narrator. They become close companions in spite of the newcomer's tendency to contradict the narrator by correcting him. His speaking voice becomes the same as Wilson's. His moral sense is keen and Wilson resents his judgments. One night he goes to play a practical joke on his companion, while the latter is sleeping. However, something he sees in the face of his sleeping companion makes him rush away in terror, never to return to the school.

He goes to Eton where he passes three years in a life of dissipation. In the midst of a wild party a stranger of exactly his size whispers in his ear the name, William Wilson. The name, of course, is his own, and reminds him of his better self. It is a voice of restraint, but Wilson will not heed it, and gods on to Oxford, where he leads an even more profligate life than before. At Oxford, although rich, he takes delight in ruining young men at cards. He is in the act of beating Lord Glendinning at cards, when into astounded company comes a stranger "closely muffled in a clack". He informs the men that Wilson has been cheating and that the evidence is in his pockets. They seize him, search him, and he is exposed. He flees to Europe in a desperate attempt to shake loose his nemesis. Again and again, however, the shadowy interloper from the past exposes him when he is about to commit a great evil. He attends a party in Rome at which he attempts to seduce the wife of the host. As he is going to meet her a figure appears out of the crowd and again he hears the hateful voice in his ear. This time, however, he drags the offender into an antechamber and kills him with his sword. He turns and to his dismay he sees in a mirror the figure of the man he has killed, himself. He perceives, finally, that he and Wilson are one. The vision in the mirror is himself, but it is the interloper as well, and as he sees the lips move he fancies that he himself is speaking the words he hears:

"You have conquered, and I yield. Yet henceforth art thou also dead-dead to the World, to Heaven, and to Hope! In me didst thou exist-and, in my death, see by this image, which is thine own, how utterly thou hast murdered thyself."

CHARACTER ANALYSES

Narrator, William Wilson

William Wilson is two men. He is the drunk, the cheat, and the seducer as well as the man who levels moral judgment against these things. Wilson is all desire, all self. He is the dark underpart of the human consciousness allowed free reign in society. With demonic energy he thrusts himself into numberless plans for self-gratification or the sadistic destruction of the other people. His is the energy of the id, in Freudian terms. He is pure energy devoted to all the wrong purposes.

The companion of his school days, the moral interloper, however, is also Wilson. He is the voice of self-denial and abnegation, the voice of morality. All his energy is directed to restraining the chaotic desires of his other self. He acts as a kind of moral break upon the headlong descent of Wilson into the pit of self-gratification, which is also the pit of hell.

To say that Poe as author was either of the William Wilsons in the tale is absurd. He was both. That is, he knew well the follies into which men may fall, partly because he could look with detachment upon his own experience, and partly because he was an intelligent man and could see the obvious shortcomings of human nature. The popular tradition about Poe's life, the one that holds he was a kind of fiend incarnate, tempts an interpretation of this story that would make Wilson's moral death a reflection of Poe's moral degeneration. However, Poe was very much alive to the moral life. He had a glimpse of the effect of selfishness upon the human soul and was horrified by what he saw. The idea that he embraced evil or sold his soul to the devil is an oversimplification.

Comment

Poe was not the first modern writer to externalize the moral division of a soul in conflict. In 1794 William Godwin had published Caleb Williams. In it a man and his conscience are embodied in the guilty Falkland and in Caleb Williams who shares his secret. Poe was familiar with Godwin's work and referred to it. Poe's handling of the **theme** in "William Wilson" had a marked influence on at least three specific literary works: Oscar Wilde's *The Picture of Dorian Gray*, Huysman's *A Rebours*, and Stevenson's *Dr. Jekyll and Mr. Hyde*.

In "William Wilson" Poe relied upon his childhood experience as a student in England at Stoke Newington. All the gothic details of the story are taken from Mr. Bransby's school at which Poe passed so many happy days. Poe had dealt with the disintegration of personality before in Roderick Usher and in the narrator of "The Black Cat." In the character of William Wilson, however, he gave the topic his most complete treatment. The tale is built around the idea of the dual nature of man, a theory of man that in its origins is religious. From the point of view of the story, when a man indulges himself he destroys himself. The spirit of selfishness which is present in all men must be kept in check or man will come a beast. Every man is given sufficient opportunity to overcome the beast in himself. Only by a conscious act of denial can a man banish the possibility of salvation. Man has free will and can choose either selfishness or selflessness. With the former comes damnation and with the latter, salvation. When Wilson kills his conscience, the only force that has prevented him from really committing himself to a life of sin, then he is lost to the world, to heaven, and to hope. The crime, which is a crime against himself, seals his damnation.

ESSAY QUESTION AND ANSWER

Question: Discuss at least two ways in which Poe maintains suspense in "William Wilson."

Answer: The most obvious way that Poe maintains suspense in the tale is by keeping the reader in doubt about the fate of Wilson. What is to become of this maniacally depraved man? The issue is in doubt until the last words of the story. The reader's interest is held high because the story is essentially a contest and the reader wants to find out who wins. The tension in the story is the tension in man. The story is dramatic because man is dramatic, always having to choose between good and evil. Wilson appears to choose evil every time, but for all the reader knows, the strange, shadowy figure that pursues Wilson may be victorious in the end.

A second way in which Poe maintains suspense in the story is through the careful manipulation of the typical props of the gothic tale. Mr. Bransby's school suggests the supernatural. The virtuous stranger also suggests the supernatural, both in what he stands for and in the manner of his operation. Connected with the **theme** of the supernatural, of course, is the true identity of the stranger. Poe drops hints along the way, but the final revelation is left for the last paragraph. Poe's true literary genius reveals itself in nothing so much as the way he is able to synthesize in one conclusion the identity of the stranger with the resolution of the simple question of what is going to happen to Wilson. He thus welds together in one indissoluble literary unit two necessaries of great fiction, interest and significance.

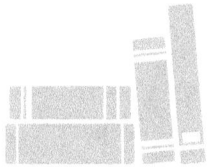

THE FALL OF THE HOUSE OF USHER

TEXTUAL ANALYSIS

CHARACTERS

Narrator

Roderick Usher

Madeline Usher

PLOT ANALYSIS

On a "dull, dark, and soundless day in the autumn of the year" the narrator travels to visit his boyhood companion, Roderick Usher. The House of Usher looks out upon a "black and lurid tarn" and is surrounded by decaying vegetation. The narrator is depressed and unnerved by his melancholy surroundings. As he peers at the image of the house in the water, he fancies there is an atmosphere peculiar to the whole area, "a pestilent and mystic vapor, dull, sluggish, faintly discernible, and leaden-hued." Before he enters the mansion he notices that its entire front is covered by minute fungi. A valet conducts him through intricate passages to the rooms of Roderick Usher, whom he finds greatly changed. His complexion is cadaverous, his eyes unusually bright, and he is suffering from "excessive nervous agitation." The morbid acuteness of his senses makes him shun food, light and sound, except in their mildest forms. His condition is complicated by the wasting away of his sister Madeline who is slowly dying of an unknown disease.

The narrator attempts to relieve the melancholy of his friend. They read and paint together, and Usher sometimes plays the guitar. The narrator realizes that he cannot cheer his friend who has obviously entered on purpose a world of strange spiritual reality. He and Madeline are the last of his line and the evil genius of the family seems to demand that they investigate modes of being that are unknown to other men. He accompanies his wild impromptus on the guitar with rhymed improvisations. One of his poems, titled "The Haunted Palace," speaks of evil things which overthrow a kingdom of wisdom and light. Usher speaks of his belief in the sentience of all vegetable life, and he cites as evidence the very fungi and decaying vegetation that attracted the narrator's attention when he first came to the House of Usher. He claims the effect of the vegetable atmosphere has molded the family and himself.

The Lady Madeline dies, and at Usher's request his friend helps him to inter the coffin temporarily in a vault in the basement of the mansion. They open the coffin for a last look at the deceased and notice "a faint blush upon the bosom and the face," a characteristic, the narrator tells us, of deaths due to catalepsis. In the days following the interment of his sister, Roderick ignores his ordinary occupations and wanders through the house aimlessly. At times he appears to be listening in profound attention to some sound that only he can hear. One stormy night the narrator is unable to sleep and Usher comes to his room in a distraught condition. He points to a window, and upon looking out his friend perceives that "a faintly luminous and distinctly visible gaseous exhalation" hangs about the mansion. In an effort to calm the hypersensitive Roderick his friend reads to him, but is interrupted by a knock at the door. Usher cries out that it is his sister at the door, whom he knows they had put living in the tomb. The Lady Madeline enters, bloody and emaciated, and falls upon her brother who dies of fright as they collapse to the floor. The narrator rushes from the mansion, and as he is riding away there is a sound "like the voice of a thousand waters," and the House of Usher sinks below the tarn.

CHARACTER ANALYSES

Narrator

The narrator in "The Fall of the House of Usher" is the controlling consciousness of the tale. The reader sees everything through his eyes. The narrator, we are led to believe, is a representative of the larger world of humanity, who had, through his friendship with Roderick Usher, been drawn into the weird world of the mansion in the tarn. The reader enters that world with him at the beginning of the story and leaves it at the end. Since he is the controlling consciousness, the reader must accept the narrator's judgment of the story's action and the characters outside himself. To the narrator Roderick Usher is both fascinating and frightening. He stays with his friend and tries to help him, never quite comprehending the extent of his involvement in supernatural speculation. He continues to the very end to play down the horrors in which he is involved, and when Usher points out the luminous mist outside the mansion he tries to explain it as an electrical phenomenon. He does not want to attribute the events of the story to forces beyond the analysis of common sense and reason. His reactions are those of the sane if less imaginative man. The reader measures the madness of Usher against the sanity of the narrator.

Roderick Usher

Roderick Usher is not a character in the ordinary sense of the word. He does not have a personality that interests the reader. Rather, it is what he has committed himself to, what he is suffering from, and his surroundings that are the focus of the story. Like so many of Poe's heroes, he is attuned to a world beyond the apprehension of ordinary men. Exactly what this world is we are never told. It is certainly for Roderick Usher a world far more real than that of everyday life. It is essentially the world of spirit, the world that is perceived by the sensitive man. Usher is a poet, a musician, and a painter. It is precisely because he is so sensitive to beauty that he knows the person outside his door is his sister. It is his intuition, his sensibility, that tells him this. Like other heroes of the romantic period, he knows what he knows immediately and by means of faculties that are superior to reason. He is the prophet, the seer, but the seer diseased and neurotic and subject to unmanly fear. What has destroyed him? It is the evil atmosphere fairly exuded by the mansion itself and the surrounding bog. Poe does not account for it; it simply exists, like evil and sin, and like evil and sin it has existed for a long time.

Madeline Usher

Madeline Usher is seen only twice in the story. Once she passes like a wraith through the room in which Roderick and his friend are reading, and causes in Usher a "more than ordinary wanness" and in the narrator "an utter astonishment not unmingled with dread." At the end of the tale we see her again as she falls upon her brother in a grisly embrace. Like her brother she is suffering from the family curse. Although the reader is not told explicitly that her strange malady is the result of the gaseous exhalation of the fungi and surrounding vegetation, the implication is clear. She is a negative character, and we see her acted upon, not acting. The assumes reader she shares her brother's interest in occult speculation, but we do not see her in depth as we do Ligeia in the story of that name.

Comment

As we have seen, many critics have interpreted Poe's tales as projections of his own situation and character, and there is undoubtedly some truth in this. Hervey Allen believes that the description of Roderick Usher might be labeled "Self Portrait of the Artist at the Age of Thirty." Critics who agree with this approach see in Usher's constitutional weakness a projection of Poe's indecisiveness and insecurity. They see in the strange curse that has fallen upon Usher a projection of Poe's feeling that he was an outcast and damned by forces beyond his control. They see repeated in Usher's unusual bond of sympathy with his sister, Poe's desire to have a woman as a perfect friend and companion with whom he could share his fears and enthusiasms.

There is, however, a limit to such an interpretation. The story stands as an independent work of art without any reference to the life of the author. The story has always been considered one of Poe's classics, and bears the characteristic marks of his craftsmanship. The House of Usher itself, with its arches and dark passageways, comes directly out of gothic horror novels, such as Horace Walpole's *Castle of Otranto*. However, if Poe often used many of the standard effects and props of the traditional horror story, he also added many of his own. The sentient fungi and gaseous exhalation are his own. Finally, it is the manner in which he handles his materials that makes Poe's tale so highly original. Everything is arranged so that the final horror will be both believable and overwhelming. Like any good showman, Poe knew how to keep his reader in suspense. The Lady Madeline's flushed cheek is the first preparation for her eventual appearance at the door. Three times as the narrator is reading to Usher a distant noise is heard, coming closer each time, before the door is finally flung open upon the final horror. A gradual, almost mathematical unfolding of plot is the very essence of Poe's art.

The **theme** of the story is the helplessness of man in the face of mysteriously evil influences beyond his control. At the core of what on the surface is merely a horror story is the idea that man lives in the presence of great evil. It is the intensity of Poe's conviction of this truth that involves the reader in what would otherwise seem an absurdly unrealistic world. Poe's particular response to this evil is one of acquiescence. The evil is too great to be challenged; it can only be experienced. Like the experience of beauty in poetry, painting and music, the experience of evil is most intense in a sensitive man like Usher. His inheritance is both good and bad. The evil that eventually overwhelms him and his sister is one part of his inheritance from the past; his superior sensitivity is the other. He has been given a nervous system capable of thrilling to both beauty and horror, and it is his evil fortune to have been given horror to thrill to instead of beauty. As in the poem that is attributed to him, the spirits of beauty and light are overcome by "vast forms" that take their life from a world of darkness and evil.

ESSAY QUESTIONS AND ANSWERS

Question: How does Poe use names and titles to develop an atmosphere of the mysterious and horrible?

Answer: Throughout the tale Poe uses exotic names and titles to evoke an atmosphere of the mysterious. We are told that Roderick Usher and his friend read together the *Directorium Inquisitorium of Eymeric de Gironne*, the *Belphegor of Machiavelli*, and the manual of a forgotten church, the *Vigiliae Mortuorum secundum Chorum Ecclesiae Maguntinae*. The titles are, to an English speaking reader, mysterious and suggestive of the supernatural. Machiavelli has always had in England and America an association with evil, and Poe makes use of this. Similarly, the Inquisition has always conjured up images of ghastly torture, an association that Poe plays upon in the title *Directorium Inquisitorium*. The technique of using exotic names and titles to evoke an atmosphere of horror has been used many times since Poe, chiefly by that modern practitioner of cosmic horror, H. P. Lovecraft. For example, in Lovecraft's "The Shadow Out of Time," he makes reference to the *Necronomicon* by the mad Arab Abdul Al Hazred for the same reason Poe has his character refer to the *Directorium*.

Question: What verbal techniques does Poe use to build in the quality of the language itself a suitable foundation for the horrible events that take place in the tale?

Answer: Poe uses **alliteration**, inversion, and rhythm to weave a pattern of language that is particularly suitable for the horror story. **Alliteration** is the repetition of the initial sound of a word, usually a consonant, in two or more words of a sentence or a line of poetry. In the first sentence the narrator tells us that the day upon which he travels to the House of Usher is "dull, dark, and soundless." Particularly in his poetry Poe uses alliteration to achieve an incantatory rhythm, the proper musical background for the weird. He uses inversion, or the reversal of the ordinary order of words in a sentence, to suggest formality, stateliness, and to draw special attention to what he is saying. He writes "I know not how it was," not "I do not know." The inverted phrase is ceremonious and suggests that the man speaking has the authority of experience behind his words. Finally, Poe's prose is far more rhythmic than the prose of most writers of fiction. He writes, for example: "It was thus that he spoke of the object of my visit, of his earnest desire to see me, and of the solace he expected me to afford him."

Even an inexperienced ear should be able to detect the repeated anapests in the first nine words of the sentence, and the carefully balanced phrases, each beginning with "of."

The texture of Poe's prose is highly poetic. The verbal techniques he is most fond of are found more often in poetry than prose. It has often been observed that his tales are in many respects more like prose-poems than stories. Short, tightly organized, and leading to a single overwhelming crisis, their organization is not unlike that of a lyric poem.

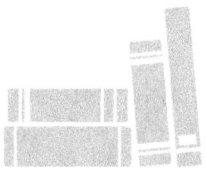

THE CONQUEROR WORM

TEXTUAL ANALYSIS

FORM

"The Conqueror Worm" is a stanzaic poem. There are five stanzas of eight lines in the poem. As in "The Haunted Palace," the lines alternate between iambic **tetrameter** and **trimeter**, with one **dimeter** line in the second stanza. Again, the **stanzas** appear to follow a standard pattern, but do not.

SUMMARY

A crowd of angels sits in a theater to see a play of hopes and fears. The actors are mere puppets that move at the bidding of "vast formless things." In the play a phantom is chased forever and the plot has to do with madness, sin, and horror. A bloody shape intrudes itself into the action. It is that of the worm. The lights go out and the curtain comes down on the tragedy "Man." The hero of the play is the worm.

Comment

"The Conqueror Worm" is related to "The Haunted Palace." In the story "Ligeia" the poem is attributed to the character of that name. Both poems were supposed to have been written by characters who have a great horror of death. What Ligeia wants more than anything else is to escape the dissolution of the body in death. The worm is symbolic of bodily decay and death. As in "The Haunted Palace," the cause of the terror is something that man does not know. The formless things are fit symbols for the unknown forces that cause, ultimately, the death of man. The play of "Man" is a tragedy because man cannot escape death. There is no salvation possible in the poem. Man is at the mercy of forces beyond his control and from which he has no appeal.

ESSAY QUESTION AND ANSWER

Question: The entire poem revolves around a central **metaphor**. What is the metaphor and how is it related to the **theme** of the poem?

Answer: The poem depends upon the idea of life being like an act. The stage has often been compared to human life. Shakespeare used the comparison in "As You Like It." In the poem life is an act, and therefore the play becomes the central **metaphor** in the poem. This metaphor is perfectly suited to convey Poe's intuition of man being subject to forces beyond his control. In a play all we can see is the actors. What goes on beyond the stage, the various forces that have been brought to bear on the actors, is unknown to us. The play, then, is an ideal **metaphor** for the communicating of the idea that man is subject to forces, nameless things, beyond his knowledge and control.

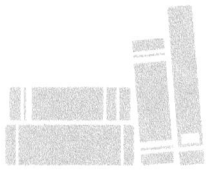

THE MURDERS IN THE RUE MORGUE

TEXTUAL ANALYSIS

CHARACTERS

Narrator

C. Auguste Dupin, a French gentleman who interests himself in crime.

PLOT ANALYSIS

The narrator distinguishes between intellectual activity characterized by mere attention, and that characterized by true acumen. Chess engages only attention and memory, and hence is not an accurate gauge of analytical power. In draughts and whist, however, besides attention and memory, the player must be able to deduce from things external to the game. He must read the faces of his opponents and be able to guess their intentions from words dropped in conversation. The truly ingenious man is always fanciful and imaginative, and never purely rational in the abstract sense.

In Paris the narrator meets Monsieur C. Auguste Dupin, a young man of aristocratic family, but limited means, who lives a retired life among his books. He arranges to live with Dupin, "in a retired and desolate portion of the Faubourg St. German." Dupin amazes the narrator by reconstructing his train of thought through occasional words dropped in conversation, and through his knowledge of his friend's character. They become interested in the murder of two women and read the newspapers avidly for news of the crime. Madame L'Espanaye and her daughter lived in a fourth floor apartment. The corpse of the daughter had been shoved up the chimney with such force that several men were required to pull it out. The corpse of the mother was found in an alley at the rear of the building with the head almost severed from the body. The apartment was in wild disorder and a fortune in gold had been abandoned on the floor. All the windows were closed and nailed from the inside and the door was locked from the inside. Several witnesses heard a Frenchman in the apartment remonstrating with someone else whose language none could identify, although there were people of many nationalities among the witnesses.

Dupin knows the Prefect of Police and gets permission to visit the scene of the crime. After his inspection he refuses to discuss the crime with his friend until the next day. The following day Dupin tells his friend that he expects at any moment a person who is implicated in the murders. While they are waiting he explains his analysis of the crime. He had concluded before examining the scene of the crime that one of the windows must have a secret latch, since the murderer must have entered in some way and could not have entered by any other means. He did in fact discover the latch his reason had led him to assume. He also discovered that one of the nails supposedly sealing a window from the inside had been broken, and only appeared to seal the window. From an inspection of the exterior of the house he concluded that someone of superhuman agility could have climbed to the window by means of a lightning rod and window shutters. The narrator suggests that an escaped maniac has committed the atrocity. Dupin claims the murderer must be an ourang-outang. He shows the narrator a notice he had placed in the newspaper, claiming that he had captured an escaped ourang-outang and would keep him until its owner called. A few minutes later a sailor appears at the door to claim the animal. Confronted with Dupin's knowledge of the crime, the sailor tells the whole story. He had captured the ourang-outang in Borneo and brought him to Paris where he escaped with a razor. He had followed the beast to the building where the crimes were committed and had climbed up the lightning rod behind the animal, from which vantage point he had remonstrated with the ourang-outang who was then in the act of murdering the two women. Upon learning of Dupin's solution of the crime, the Prefect of Police is both surprised and jealous. Dupin concludes that the Prefect is too cunning to be profound.

CHARACTER ANALYSES

Narrator

The narrator is a man who delights in the unusual. He has come to Paris to indulge himself in his fancy for the odd. He, like Dupin, is interested in rare books and genealogy. He delights in their seclusion and their friendship. In the evening they sally forth into the city, "roaming far and wide until a late hour, seeking amid the wild lights and shadows of the populous city, that infinity of mental excitement which quiet observation can afford."

Auguste Dupin

Had Poe created no other character than Dupin he would be remembered in literary history, for Dupin in the first famous detective of literature. With him Poe created a character type that now includes such famous sleuths as Sherlock Holmes, Hercule Poirot, and Perry Mason. In Dupin, Poe expressed an aspect of his own personality he had only expressed briefly before in "The Gold Bug," his fascination for fact and logical analysis. Dupin, however, is not just a man of great rational powers. We are told specifically that the narrator is attracted by "the wild fervor, and the vivid freshness of his imagination." Nevertheless, what is fascinating about Dupin is his ability to unravel the twisted threads of human action and motivation on the basis of facts alone, and his supreme imagination which enables him to draw human conclusions from abstract facts. Dupin, like so many of Poe's heroes, is a man withdrawn from the world, an intellectual who takes his mental sustenance from the exotic and peculiar. Above all else he is aware, he is conscious. What makes him able to solve mysteries the Prefect of Police cannot solve is his greater consciousness. He sees what others do not see. In his own way Poe was just as fascinated with the idea of a superman as Nietzsche and Dostoevski. His superman, however, has no desire to alter human society. In fact, his superman is seldom conscious of human society at all, so wrapped up is he in his own peculiar investigations and mental life. When he does involve himself in society it is to satisfy a whim, or to solve a problem that no one else has been able to solve. Only then does the solitary deign to involve himself in the practical world of everyday life.

Comment

There are several important sources for "The Murders in the Rue Morgue." In the autumn of 1838, Burton's Magazine published as a serial the "Unpublished Passages in the Life of Vidocq, the French Minister of Police." Poe had always been interested in crime, and read the series. The ourang-outang was suggested by Sir Walter Scott's *Count Robert of Paris* in which the chattering of an ourang-outang is mistaken for the voice of someone speaking in an unknown language. According to W. E. Waller, Poe may have seen an extract from the *Shrewsbury Chronicle* for July, 1834. It told of traveling showmen who had brought a baboon to town, which they had taught to commit robberies by climbing up great heights. From these materials Poe constructed "The Murders in the Rue Morgue."

More important than the story in itself as a work of art, however, is the basic conception behind it of a man of intelligence and sophistication who helps the police in the solution of crimes they cannot unravel. The conception was, in fact, the beginning of modern detective fiction. It is rare that a man both creates a form and excels in it, yet this is exactly what Poe did. "The Murders in the Rue Morgue" and its two sequels, "The Mystery of Marie Roget" and "The Purloined Letter," are among the classics of their kind. Central to the idea is the admiring friend and assistant who is less intelligent than the mastermind, perhaps even bumbling like Sherlock Holmes' Dr. Watson, yet always a loyal and devoted companion. Together they accomplish what the authorities are unable to accomplish. The Prefect of Police provides a kind of wry humor through his unsuccessful efforts which are obviously doomed to failure from the beginning.

The detective story as Poe created it was particularly well designed for continued action and for continued interest on the part of the reading audience. From story to story the possibilities are almost limitless, as broad, certainly, as human nature itself in the number and variety of crimes possible, and the methods of their execution and solution. Poe himself only scratched the surface of the form he had created. It remained for Sir Arthur Conan Doyle to realize fully the possibilities of the detective story. This he did in two ways, both suggested by Poe. First he created two characters interesting in their own right, and then conceived of them involved in series of **episodes** all centering around the detection of crime, but in themselves enormously varied. Inspector Lestrade of Scotland Yard took the place of the Prefect of Police as the inefficient authority whom the mastermind would always outwit by the final page. Poe, then, was the intellectual father of characters as far removed from his world as Charlie Chan. Nor does the form show any indication of a quick demise. Like any form, however, it will take truly great artists to realize its possibilities.

ESSAY QUESTIONS AND ANSWERS

Question: When the narrator returns to Dupin on the morning after their investigation of the scene of the murder, Dupin describes in a long narrative how he solved the mystery. How does Poe keep the reader's attention during this rather long section in which there is no action?

Answer: Poe keeps the reader's attention in two ways, one depending on essentially intellectual interest, and one depending on pure emotion. In Dupin's narrative Poe has him proceed from fact to fact in the solution of the crime, and the reader follows to see where he is going, to see how all the facts tie together. The narrator's guess that the murderer is an escaped maniac marks the chief transition in the narrative, after which the true nature of the murder is revealed. When the narrator first arrives in Dupin's apartment, Dupin tells him that he expects at any moment the arrival of a man who is involved in the crime. As Dupin's narrative progresses the reader knows that the arrival of the unknown person is coming closer and closer. The suspense created by this knowledge is purely emotional, and yet parallels the unfolding of Dupin's story. Intellectual interest in the solution of the mystery, and suspense due to the momentary arrival of the unknown party thus develop together.

Question: What aspect of the crime first gives Dupin a clue to its solution?

Answer: That which gives Dupin a clue to the true nature of the crime is exactly what prompts the police to claim the mystery cannot be solved, namely "the outre Character of its features." When faced with the unusual the police thrown up their hands in dismay, whereas Dupin discovers in the unusual an aid to solution. Instead of asking himself what has happened, he asks himself what has happened that has never happened before, and then proceeds to construct a theory that will explain the facts that are so unusual. It is in the construction of the theory of the crime that his imagination comes into play, whereas his analytical reason bears the greatest burden in simply observing the facts and listing, as it were, the separate elements of the crime that are unusual. Poe was too much of a poet to allow any of his heroes to be completely rational. Dupin has the mind of a mathematician and the soul of a poet. It is this unusual combination of qualities that makes him the success that he is.

DREAM-LAND

TEXTUAL ANALYSIS

FORM

"Dream-Land" is a lyric poem of five sections. The sections are 8, 12, 18, 12, and 6 lines respectively. The poem is written in **trochaic** tetrameter couplets. There are four accents in each line and the lines begin, for the most part, with accented syllables. In the third section the tenth line is cast in iambic dimeter.

SUMMARY

By a lonely and obscure route haunted by bad angels and ruled by the phantom or image called Night, the poet has reached the world of dreams. It is beyond space and time. It is a land of lonely lakes and swamps, deep canyons, and restless seas. Memories of the past walk the land. For the restless and unhappy heat it is a peaceful region. However, no traveler can view the mysteries of the place directly. The souls that pass through it must view it through darkened glasses.

Comment

"Dream-Land" is similar to "The City in the Sea" in that both are period pieces. That is, they deal with **themes** that are suggested more by the official literary life of the day than by intense personal experience. The details of the poem, the ghouls, and sheeted memories, come directly out of the gothic horror tales. The versification is competent, and the technique of a really good writer has made of this poem an enduring piece when hundreds like it would be almost unreadable today.

ESSAY QUESTION AND ANSWER

Question: Discuss the first and last **stanzas** in their structural relationships to the rest of the poem.

Answer: The first **stanza** is introductory. It speaks of the chief quality of the world of dreams, namely that it is beyond space and time. It also describes the arrival of the poet in dreamland. The **stanza**, then, fulfills quite adequately the necessities of an introductory **stanza**. Poe was absolutely intent upon the need for structure in poetry as well as in fiction. When the reader finished a poem Poe wanted him to have the feeling that he was indeed finished, that he had experienced a beginning, a middle, and an end. When Poe came to conclude "Dream-Land" he used the technique of repeating with slight alteration in the last **stanza** the exact statements he used in the first **stanza**. In the first stanza he wrote of dreamland: "I have reached these lands but newly." In the last **stanza** he wrote: "I have wandered home but newly." By concluding with a slight variation of what he used in the first **stanza** he gives the reader the feeling of having been somewhere and returned, of having begun and completed an action.

THE MASQUE OF THE RED DEATH

TEXTUAL ANALYSIS

CHARACTERS

Prince Prospero

Lords And Ladies

PLOT ANALYSIS

A plague had devastated the country and no other pestilence could compare with its horror. Within half an hour the victim ran the entire course of the disease from sharp pains and dizziness to bleeding at the pores and, finally, death. Prince Prospero is happy in spite of the plague, and summons a thousand lords and ladies to the deep seclusion of one of his abbeys. The building is a product of the Prince's own eccentric taste and is filled with exotic ornaments. It is sealed from the outside world by an enormous wall with gates of iron. In the society within there were buffoons, dancers, musicians, and all that one could desire to pass the time pleasantly. They intend to stay secluded until the plague has run its course.

In the sixth month of their seclusion the Prince decides to hold a masked ball. It is to be held in an imperial suite of seven rooms. Each apartment is irregular to satisfy the Prince's love of the bizarre, and the eye cannot see for more than thirty yards before the room turns in another direction. At each turn of the wall a narrow gothic window looks out on a closed corridor. Opposite each window there is a brazier of fire that shines through the tinted glass and illuminates the rooms in an eerie manner. Each room is decorated in a single color and the last is red. In the red apartment stands a gigantic ebony clock that strikes the hours with a heavy, monotonous clang.

The apartments are densely crowded for the ball. At the stroke of midnight a guest is observed in the costume of the red death itself, and horrifies the guests. The Prince is angered at what appears to be a practical joke in poor taste. He orders the stranger seized and hanged at sunrise from the battlements. He is pursued into the red chamber where he is seized in the shadow of the ebony clock. The Prince is the first in pursuit, and a few feet from the figure falls dead. Other seize the unknown person in the outre costume, and to their horror find there is no living form in the animated death weeds. One by one the revelers die until they are all dead, and death is the king of all.

CHARACTER ANALYSES

Prince Prospero

Prince Prospero is a figure from the world of fairy. As an allegorical type he does not have personality in the same sense that a character in a realistic story would have. He represents a type, the man of total indulgence who seeks to avoid all the misfortunes and limitations of human life. He is uncompromisingly selfish and uses all the power at his command simply to satisfy his whims. In matters of artistic taste he is, like so many of Poe's heroes, a child of the gothic horror story, resembling the title character of William Beckford's Vathek more than anyone else.

Lords And Ladies

The lords and ladies of "The Masque of the Red Death" are, like Prince Prospero, without personality. Like fantastically costumed wraiths, they flit through the apartments of the royal suite, emblems of a social order long since decayed even in Poe's day. There are inhabitants of Poe's city of Babylon, occupying themselves in perpetual revel until the heavy hand of death falls upon them.

Comment

It may appear a truism to say that Poe's tales are unrealistic, and yet such an observation is necessary to appreciate their unique quality. The twentieth-century reader has been conditioned to fiction whose chief goal is the accurate representation of the life of the world. It concentrates on the relationships of men with each other and their struggle to succeed in life. The novel, of course, has always been associated with **realism**. One of the first novels, *Robinson Crusoe*, was a triumph of **realism**, and Poe admired it as one of the truly great books. It was generally accepted, however, that under the category of romance a writer was freed from the restrictions imposed on the novelist. The writer of romance was allowed such liberties in order to more accurately dramatize and communicate the truths of the heart. In his preface to *The House of the Seven Gables*, Nathaniel

Hawthorne wrote one of the classic definitions of romance. He spoke of the liberties available to the writer of romance:

> If he think fit, also, he may so manage his atmospherical medium as to bring out or mellow the lights and deepen and enrich and shadows of the picture. He will be wise, no doubt, to make a very moderate use of the privileges here stated, and, especially, to mingle the Marvellous rather as a slight, delicate, and evanescent flavor, than as any portion of the actual substance of the dish offered to the public. He can hardly be said, however, to commit a literary crime even if he disregard this caution.

Hawthorne's own stories were allegories of the heart, and Poe was the first major writer to praise Hawthorne's *Twice Told Tales*, in a review that is now a classic.

"The Masque of the Red Death" is a romance. The masque of the title is a masquerade or masked ball. It was a form of entertainment popular with the aristocracy in sixteenth and seventeenth century England, and was characterized by lavish costumes, music, scenery, and dialogue. Poe was not known for his moderation in any human activity, and did not observe Hawthorne's advice to mingle the Marvellous" as a flavor throughout the work. There is not one sentence of the story that is not touched with the marvelous. It is pure imagination from beginning to end. As an allegory the tale is strangely reminiscent of the morality plays of the Middle Ages. The moral is not, perhaps, as explicitly clear as that of Everyman, the most famous of the English morality plays, and yet it is there. The inevitability of death, the folly of pride, the impossibility of preserving life against the evils of the world-all these ideas are at the heart of the story. Perhaps the central theme is that of appearance and reality. What appears to be real, the glittering society of the abbey, is in reality an illusion. The reality is death which reigns triumphant at the end of the tale.

    Poe finished "The Masque of the Red Death" in 1842, at about the same he was working on "The Mystery of Marie Roget" and "The Pit and the Pendulum." The violence of the tale and Poe's obsession with blood are no doubt traceable to the fact that only a few months before he engaged himself in the story Virginia had had a particularly bad attack in which a blood vessel had burst. At best Poe had a nervous disposition, and his wife's affliction rendered him unfit for his ordinary editorial labors. Toward the end of June Poe left home under unusual psychological pressure and went to New Jersey where he looked up a former sweetheart, Mary Devereaux. He behaved with great violence, and several passengers on the ferry took him to be a lunatic. He was finally found by Mrs. Clemm wandering in the woods on the edge of town. Although it is not always possible to establish an exact relationship between Poe's life and his fiction, it is certainly safe to say that the agony of soul that was so often his lot to endure is communicated in his tales, and accounts for their imaginative intensity.

ESSAY QUESTIONS AND ANSWERS

Question: What does the clock symbolize in the story and how is it used to reinforce the main **theme** of the tale?

Answer: The gigantic ebony clock with its monotonous pendulum symbolizes the transiency of human life and the inevitability of death. It is black, a color that has always suggested decay and dissolution. Whenever it strikes the hour, the peculiar nature of its tone disturbs the revelers and makes them grow pale. However, they are able to ignore it until the appearance of the mysterious masker just after the clock strikes twelve. The Prince dies in the shadow of the clock and the merrymakers, seizing the grim visitor, find the costume to be empty of any form. The clock, then, comes to symbolize all in the outside world that the highborn ladies and lords have sought to escape.

Question: In the last paragraph of the tale Poe uses just about every rhetorical technique available to the writer of prose. Name some of them and give examples.

Answer: He uses inversion. He writes "and died each," not "and each died." He uses **simile**, as in the sentence "He came like a thief in the night." He uses **alliteration** in the last sentence, "And Darkness and Decay and the Red Death held illimitable dominion over all." He uses repetition. All but one sentence in the paragraph begins with "and." He uses rhythm, particularly in the fourth sentence, "And the life of the ebony clock went out with that of the last of the gay." The paragraph, in short, is a virtuoso performance. It could only have been written by a poet.

THE RAVEN

TEXTUAL ANALYSIS

FORM

"The Raven" is a stanzaic poem. There are eighteen stanzas in the poem, each consisting of six lines. The first five lines of each **stanza** are written in **trochaic** octameter, that is, the accent falls on the first syllable and there are eight accents or beats in each line. The sixth line, the **refrain**, is written in **trochaic tetrameter**, with four accents to the line. The last three lines of each **stanza rhyme**. Poe uses internal rhyme in the first and third lines of each **stanza**. The fourth accented syllable **rhymes** with the eighth accepted syllable in both the first and the third lines of each **stanza**. The **stanzas** are elaborate in their form, bound together by full **rhyme**, internal **rhyme**, and a refrain.

SUMMARY

At midnight the "I" or consciousness of the poem is reading old books in a melancholy mood. He is sorrowing for his lost lover Lenore. He hears a tapping at the chamber door. He thinks to himself that only a visitor is at the door, but when the tapping persists he flings the door open. All he hears is the echo of the word "Lenore." He sees nothing and so closes the door, but the tapping immediately begins again. He opens a shutter and in walks a stately raven that says nothing, but perches on a bust of Pallas above the door. He asks the bird its name, but all the animal replies to his entreaties is "nevermore." The ungainly and somber bird beguiles the poet into smiling. However, the bird drives the poet into a frenzy by its mindless repetition of one word. He asks the bird if he will meet Lenore in the next world, but as usual the raven replies "nevermore." He directs the bird to leave his room and go back into the night, but the raven will not move. The bird is still sitting on the bust at the end of the poem, and he now has the aspect of a demon. The poet says his soul will never escape the shadow of the raven.

Comment

"The Raven" is the most famous poem that Poe ever wrote, although it is certainly not his best. He was often asked to recite the poem and for a while he himself was referred to as "the raven." The poem is remarkable both in its form and in the way the poet is able to build the human speaking voice into the poem. The form of the poem is unusual. A line with eight accents is rather long to handle successfully in English, but Poe is able to modify the staccato beat with mellifluous and alliterating words. Perhaps the most unusual feature of the poem is its incorporation of the human speaking voice. The voice is not quite conversational, because the emotional pitch of the poem is too high to be called conversational. The voice is that of a man speaking out loud, but to himself. The voice is alternately depressed, angry, and resigned. It gives the poem a sense of unfolding drama.

One school of critics maintains that "The Raven" is a literary joke, but the more conventional interpretation has the poet intending the poem to be taken seriously. There is an element of truth in the idea that the poem is a joke, or that there is a rich vein of humor in the poem. Certainly the initial entrance of the raven is without a doubt humorous, The stateliness and soberness of the bird in entering the window must provoke at least mirth. As well as the basic situation, some of the individual lines are humorous. When the poet addresses the bird as "Sir" and "Madam" he obviously intends a whimsical humor. The poem, then, is both humorous and serious at the same time. The quixotic nature of Poe's imagination accounts for the variety of moods in the poem. He was too mentally quick to be satisfied with registering a single response to a situation, and the result is that the meaning of the raven changes as the imaginative context of the poem changes. On the whole, however, the poem is meant to be taken seriously.

ESSAY QUESTIONS AND ANSWERS

Question: Discuss the changes in the mood of the "I" of the poem. How do they modify the emotional tone of the poem?

Answer: At the beginning of the poem the poet is in a melancholy mood. He has lost his lover and is pensive because of his loss. The raven beguiles the poet into a wry humor by its absurd appearance. However, when the bird replies nothing but "nevermore" to his questions, the poet becomes angry with the bird. From anger the mood of the poem is deepened into hatred and despair. His lover will never come back, and the bird perched above his door and so mindlessly croaking becomes a fit symbol for both his loss and his outcast state. So many changes of mood in a relatively short poem make the poem dramatic. The reader is not kept upon the same emotional level, but is shifted up and down as the poet's mood changes.

THE PIT AND THE PENDULUM

TEXTUAL ANALYSIS

CHARACTERS

Narrator

PLOT ANALYSIS

The narrator is "sick unto death," and when he hears the dread sentence of death passed upon him he faints away. He sees but faintly the black-robed judges of the Inquisition. His sense impressions are blurred and kaleidoscopic. In a state of only semiconsciousness the narrator is aware of a descent into darkness. It seems interminable and he becomes dizzy. When he awakes fully he can see nothing but "the blackness of eternal night." The atmosphere is close and he has to lie quietly to focus his thoughts. He dreads to move lest he discover only the walls of a tomb. He does attempt to explore his dungeon, however, and as he does so he remembers all that had been whispered about the horrors of Toledo. He encounters a wall that is slimy, smooth, and cold. Overcome with exhaustion, he falls down and lapses into sleep.

When he awakes he discovers that bread and water have been left for him, and he eats. Again he attempts to explore the dungeon and again he falls. He feels nothing under his head and smells an abominable smell of decayed fungus. A pit is directly in front of him and he draws back, shaking with horror. He discovers the walls of the prison are metal and covered with the images of fiends. He sleeps, and when he wakes he finds himself bound with a strap. As he looks upward he is able to see the ceiling of the prison for the first time, and it appears to be in motion. The figure of Time is painted on the ceiling, but instead of a scythe the figure bears a huge pendulum which is swinging back and forth directly above him. It appears to be made of a crescent of sharp steel. Huge rats creep out of the pit and watch him from the brink. He decides that his torturers have presented him with two possibilities for death, the pit or the pendulum. The pendulum descends toward him very slowly. A plan of escape comes to him. As the sharp pendulum cuts through his bonds he will slip to safety. He wonders what food the rats have been fed upon in the hideous pit. The pendulum comes ceaselessly down. As it slices within inches of his body the strap is cut and he is freed.

As he is freed the pendulum is withdrawn toward the ceiling. A light seems to be illuminating the cell. He realizes that the dungeon is being heated. As the metal begins to glow the faces of the fiends on the wall contort horribly. It becomes hotter and hotter and he thinks of plunging into the pit, all the while knowing that that is what his tormentors want him to do. The cell begins to contract, forcing him closer and closer to the pit. Finally, he is forced to the ultimate verge and screams in despair. At that moment there is a blast of trumpets and the walls roll back. Arms lift him from the cell. He learns that General Lasalle and the French army have entered Toledo.

CHARACTER ANALYSES

Narrator

The narrator, as so often happens in Poe's tales, is completely passive. We see him acted upon, not acting. He is not simply acted upon by evil men who want to torture him to death. The narrator is innocent, and as such a kind of literary guinea pig. Poe begins his tale with the innocent narrator being acted upon. He then keeps the reader's interest through the various tortures that the narrator must endure. Whatever Poe's imagination contrives for the narrator to suffer, the reader experiences it also, at a distance. Interest in the narrator depends in part on a curiosity that is not entirely healthy. The reader wants to see what happens to the narrator and be thrilled by the various horrors he has to undergo. The narrator has no personality, no character. He exists only as an instrument, a gauge upon which can be registered the effects of the grotesque tortures that Poe dreams up for him to endure.

In one respect alone does the narrator of "The Pit and the Pendulum" resemble Poe himself. Like Poe, he is unusually aware of what is happening to him. Every feeling, every sight pierces him to the marrow, so that he is constantly being battered by succeeding waves of impressions. Poe succeeded in projecting the quality of his own personality without any of its contents. That is, we never learn anything of the narrator's likes of dislikes, nor are we ever introduced to his full humanity.

Comment

"The Pit and the Pendulum" is a story of adventure and suspense. It does not attempt more than the entertainment of the reader, but it accomplishes that with a particular excellence and a flare for the dramatic that is characteristic of Poe. The first sentence of the story projects the reader into the heart of the action and he remains there until the conclusion of the story. "I was sick-sick unto death with that long agony; and when they at length unbound me, and I was permitted to sit, I felt that my senses were leaving me." With that first sentence the reader is introduced to a world of incredibly acute sense impressions, impressions of evil, horror, and death. Poe was able to describe sense impressions with such intensity that he could almost depend upon them alone to sustain the reader's interest in the story. The tale is contrived not around a plot that is self-sustaining, but rather the tenuous thread of the plot is constructed to provide Poe with the opportunity of indulging in a perfect riot of sense impressions. Sight, smell, hearing, touch and taste-not one is neglected. It is intensely dark and the narrator strains to see. He discovers that the walls and floor of the dungeon are covered with slime by touching them. The terrible silence weighs on his ears and every sound seems magnified. He smells the fetid pit with its decaying fungi. He is tortured by thirst. The food he is given is hot on purpose to drive him to an act of self destruction in the abominable pit.

It is not enough, however, to say that Poe directs himself to sense impressions in this tale. He does more. He is able to evoke the impressions of a man in a state of psychological and physical collapse. At the beginning of the tale, when he is still before the judges, he sees seven tall candles. In his delirium they appear first as "white, slender angels" who have come to save him. In his shattered consciousness they next loom up as "meaningless specters, with heads of flame" before they disappear and he sinks into the darkness of the tomb.

The technique of the story cannot be reduced to simply a sum of various sense impressions, however. Lying behind all the impressions is always the question of what, ultimately, will happen. Will the narrator survive? Will he meet a hideous end in front of the reader's eyes? What new horrors will he experience? In short, the tale is based upon one of the oldest techniques in story telling, that of manipulated suspense. Poe had mastered the drama of suspense by the time he came to write "The Pit and the Pendulum." He does not make one false move, but keeps the reader in constant suspense. At times it seems that the narrator will escape, but his hopes are dashed. At times it seems as if he must perish instantly, but he does not. Where is he? What is to become of him" Poe allows all these questions to develop in the reader's mind. He prolongs the suspense until almost the last sentence of the story, and has the narrator rescued just as he is about to plunge into the pit. The conclusion is similar to that of "MS. Found in a Bottle," particularly in its constructions. In both tales the reader must wait until the very end before the suspense ends, although in "The Pit and the Pendulum" the narrator is rescued while in "MS. Found in a Bottle" he is not.

ESSAY QUESTION AND ANSWER

Question: In many of Poe's tales the hero is concerned about life after death. It is a consistent **theme** in his more important work. Is this theme discussed in any way in "The Pit and the Pendulum"? How is this **theme** related to Poe's technique in the tale?

Answer: At the very beginning of the tale, when the narrator faints, his sensations while unconscious are compared to those of delirium and death. He is led to the observation that consciousness can never be completely lost. He writes: "In death-no! even in the grave all is not lost." He goes on to say that were there a state in which all consciousness faded away, it would mean that the soul is not immortal. This observation is related to Poe's technique in the story. If there is no state in which consciousness fades completely, then the sensitive man will always feel something, always think something. This enlarges the scope of the tale. Poe can devote himself to all the nuances of thought and feeling that the narrator experiences as he awakens and discovers the full extent of his predicament.

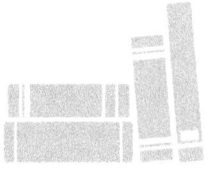

THE MYSTERY OF MARIE ROGET

TEXTUAL ANALYSIS

CHARACTERS

Narrator

Dupin

PLOT ANALYSIS

The narrator says that even the calmest thinkers have at times given a kind of half-assent to the supernatural by coincidences of a seemingly marvelous character. Such feelings are never completely stifled unless the thinker involved refers to the Calculus of Probabilities.

After the solving of the murders in the Rue Morgue, Dupin lapses into his former life. He is not able, however, to enjoy the complete anonymity of his former life, as his success in solving the murders has made him famous. The Prefect of Police requests his help in the case of Marie Roget. The girl had disappeared from the shop of a perfumer which she had made famous by her beauty and charm. About a week later the girl returned, and it was given out that she had been visiting a relative in the country. Five months after her first disappearance she was again missed, and after four days her body was found floating in the Seine. The youth and beauty of the victim cause extreme excitement in the city. Marie left her mother's house at nine in the morning on Sunday, June 22. She told her intended, Jacques St. Eustache, that she was going to visit her aunt. Her body was discovered by a fisherman four days later and identified by a friend. Marks on the wrists of the corpse indicated that it had been pulled some distance by a rope. A piece of material had been torn from the skirt and tied around the waist in a sailor's knot, forming a kind of halter. Many rumors are circulated concerning the murder. Some newspapers suggest the body was not Marie's and that she is still alive. Some suggest that four days are not sufficient for a body to rise from the bottom of the river, and, therefore, the corpse could not be Marie Roget. In a thicket across the river two boys discover a parasol, gloves, and a handkerchief bearing the name of Marie. Fragments of a garment strewn around indicate a struggle. The general opinion is that she was the victim of a gang of desperadoes. The narrator helps Dupin sift the newspapers for information pertaining to the crime.

Dupin indicates that a body thrown into the water after death does not sink at all, let alone require four days to rise. He concludes that the corpse found was indeed that of Marie. It is discovered that during the week of her first absence Marie was in the company of a young naval officer. Dupin concludes there must be a connection between the two disappearances, and that they are not coincidental. He decides that the handkerchief found by the boys was planted, because all the items were arranged as if a not too intelligent person had wanted it to appear that a struggle had taken place. He comes to the conclusion that she must have been the victim of an individual, since there would have been no need to pull the body if a gang had been involved, and the cloth tied around the waist was there for the purpose of pulling. The inevitable conclusion is that Marie Roget was murdered by a sailor with whom she had run off in the past. Her retaining her fiance was only a ruse to cover up her true love, and her telling him where she was going was simply a device to hide her true destination. The narrator concludes that by seeking truth simply in the amassing of details, many errors are committed. What is necessary is to find a pattern which will explain even those facts which seem to be coincidences, and link them in a reconstruction of what actually happened.

CHARACTER ANALYSES

Dupin

Dupin's performance in "The Mystery of Marie Roget" is purely mental. In "The Murders in the Rue Morgue," it was necessary for him to visit the scene of the crime in order to obtain the facts necessary to solve the crime. In the affair of Marie Roget, Dupin does not leave his study. He is able to reconstruct the crime simply as an intellectual and intuitive exercise. This is more amenable to his character than rooting around for a multitude of facts. Basically he is a recluse, and only when it is absolutely necessary will he go into the world. The solution of Marie Roget's murder, then, suits his character perfectly. He seizes upon the newspapers with avidity, and because the crime is so well discussed in all its aspects, he is able to find out all he needs to know in order to solve the crime without leaving his room.

Narrator

The narrator once again functions as Dupin's friend and assistant. In this story his chief employment is searching through the newspapers for news of the murder and for any items that might throw light on the mystery. The narrator also busies himself in confirming Dupin's intuitions. By checking affidavits he is able to confirm St. Eustache's innocence. It had been suggested that he might be the murderer.

Comment

"The Mystery of Marie Roget" was first published in 1842. It appeared as a three-part serial in the Ladies Companion. It was based on an actual murder. Mary Cecilia Rogers had disappeared in August of 1841 from a tobacconist's shop on Liberty Street in New York where she worked. Rumor had it that she had been seen in Weehawken, New Jersey, in the company of a sailor. As in the story, the common conclusion was that she had been a victim of a criminal gang. Poe was convinced the press was mistaken and solved the mystery, like Dupin, on the basis of information he was able to glean from the newspapers.

Poe set his story in Paris. The reasons for this are obvious. He had already created the character of Dupin and could not very well bring Dupin to New York, so he brought the crime to Dupin. In the story, Nassau Street, where Cecilia lived, becomes the Rue Pavee St. Andree, Weehawken becomes the Barriere du Roule, and the Hudson appears as the Seine.

The story indicates the extent to which Poe's imagination was quick to seize upon the raw material at hand and rework it in his fiction. As early as "The Gold Bug" he had given expression to his fascination for analysis. In the terminology of the day, such tales were known as tales of ratiocination. The world simply means reasoning. For fact and atmosphere in "The Gold Bug" he relied upon his childhood experiences in looking for shells on the shore near Fort Moultrie. Upon a foundation of fact Poe erected a superstructure of plot that reveals his true originality. In the same way, the facts involved in the murder of Cecilia Rogers provided Poe with the foundation for "The Mystery of Marie Roget." The existence of Dupin, his own creation, immediately suggested a manner of exploiting these facts. Given such an outline, the full development of the tale must have been a matter of pure pleasure to him.

Perhaps Poe's greatest triumph in "The Mystery of Marie Roget" is the manner in which he has Dupin reconstruct imaginatively the frame of mind of the murderer on the basis of facts alone.

The fury of his passion is over, and there is abundant room in his heart for the natural awe of the deed. His is none of that confidence which the presence of numbers inevitably inspires. He is alone with the dead. He trembles and is bewildered.

In such a passage Poe achieves a psychological insight possible only to truly fine writers, and of course the insight becomes Dupin's. Under the master's touch Dupin becomes a man of poetic as well as scientific understanding. In Dupin Poe laid the foundation for characterization in depth that was never quite realized because he was to use Dupin in only one more tale, "The Purloined Letter." Sir Arthur Conan Doyle was to benefit greatly from Poe's Dupin, however, in spite of what Sherlock Holmes says of Dupin at the beginning of "A Study in Scarlet." In the well-developed characterization of Sherlock Holmes we can see a triumph that was at least partly Poe's.

ESSAY QUESTIONS AND ANSWERS

Question: What is Dupin's attitude toward public opinion? Why doesn't he pay more attention to public opinion in this case?

Answer: Dupin tells us that in certain conditions public opinion must not be overlooked. The public opinion, however, must manifest itself in a strictly spontaneous manner. When it does it functions in the body politic like intuition in a man of genius. It is important, however, that there be no hint of suggestion in the reaction of the public. That is, the public must not have been subject to any powerful suggestion, or its first impulse will not be pure and hence will not be accurate. Dupin does not follow public opinion in the case of Marie Roget, because the public had been subject to strong suggestion. First the body of a popular and lovely lady is found in a mutilated condition. This alone aroused the people. Almost immediately afterward it was learned that another young lady had been attacked, though not killed, by a gang of desperadoes operating in almost the same area where Marie Roget was killed. The inevitable public reaction was that a gang had also been responsible for the death of Marie. Since public opinion had been seriously affected by strong suggestion, Dupin discounts it in the present case.

Question: In Dupin's opinion, is the case of Marie Roget more or less difficult than that of the murders in the Rue Morgue? What is the basis for his opinion?

Answer: Dupin thinks that the mystery of Marie Roget is more difficult than the murders in the Rue Morgue. The Rue Morgue case seemed difficult because it was so outre. However, precisely because it was so outre it was easy to solve, presenting, as it did, so many unusual facts that pointed toward an inevitable conclusion. The case of Marie is terrible but utterly common.

Not one outre detail is presented in the entire picture. Precisely because this is true many people expect a quick solution to the case, but in Dupin's analysis it will be difficult because it is common.

THE BLACK CAT

TEXTUAL ANALYSIS

CHARACTERS

Narrator

PLOT ANALYSIS

The narrator assures the reader that he is not mad. He tells in brief the story of his life. As a child he had a tender heart and was fond of animals. He married early and found in his wife a congenial disposition. They kept all sorts of pets, including a cat named Pluto. The animal was entirely black and noted for its intelligence. His wife was superstitious and suggested the animal was a witch in disguise, as the Egyptians believed, a view the narrator ridiculed. He became addicted to alcohol and his temper became worse and worse. His entire personality experienced a degeneration. One night as he returned home, completely drunk, he was possessed by the fury of a demon, seized the cat, and cut out one of its eyes. He was filled with remorse and attempted to drown his sorrow in wine. In a spirit of perverseness he hangs the cat from a tree because he knows that in doing so he is committing an awful sin. A spirit of contradiction forces him to do the opposite of what he knows to be right. On the very night of the evil deed his house burns down and he is left destitute. Burnt into the one remaining wall of the house is the figure of a gigantic cat.

In a den of infamy the narrator finds a cat that looks just like Pluto. He even has one eye missing, but instead of being completely black, he has a white spot on his chest. He takes the animal home. Remorse, shame, and bitterness drive him to hate the cat. As his hatred for the animal increases, its affection for him increases. The white spot on the cat's chest begins to assume the shape of a gallows. One day while working in the basement he is goaded into fury by the animal and is about to kill it with an axe when his wife intervenes. Furious at her interference, he buries the axe in her brain. All his attention is then applied to concealing the corpse. The cellar had recently been plastered. He removes part of the wall and interns the body of his wife in an upright position. He looks for the cat that prompted the crime, but cannot find it.

He is filled with a sense of enormous relief. Four days after the crime the police come to inspect the house. They search the basement, but find nothing. As they are going up the stairs the spirit of perverseness in the narrator drives him to rap on the wall with his cane, just where he had interred the body. In a complete frenzy of bravado he asks them if it is not a well-made house. A sound answers him from the wall, "a wailing shriek, half of horror and half of triumph, such as might have arisen only out of hell, conjointly from the throats of the damned in their agony, and of the demons that exult in the damnation." The men tear down the wall and find the corpse "already greatly decayed and clotted with gore." Upon its head is sitting the missing cat, staring at them balefully from its one eye.

CHARACTER ANALYSES

Narrator

By nature the narrator has an affectionate, kindly temperament. His addiction to liquor, however, develops in him a tendency to schizophrenia. One moment he will be in a perfect frenzy of violence, with nothing but curses and vituperation even for those he loves. Very quickly, however, he is overcome with remorse and is sorry for all that he has said and done. The two cats remind him of what he was in better days, and he cannot endure their presence. What particularly goads him are those things for which he formerly had great affection. He becomes solitary and shuns both animals and men. He appears powerless to alter his condition, and yet he does have moments of extreme remorse and guilt. In the narrator we see a man driven by sullen hatred of himself, which of course leads to hatred of everything. He cannot stand anyone else because they require him to come out of himself, but in a sullen, introverted fury he refuses to do so. He will not be sane or happy.

He is afraid of the second cat, and fear is added to a mental state already confused and dangerous. He becomes excessively nervous and has difficulty controlling himself. It is this tendency that proves his undoing. Like the narrator of "The Premature Burial," once an idea or impulse comes to him he cannot prevent it from running its course. He cannot resist the temptation to lead the police to the very spot in the wall behind which the corpse is interred. His quixotic imagination cannot be controlled, and aware of the **irony** of the situation, he cannot help rapping on the very spot with his cane. He is a picture of a character in total disintegration.

Comment

"The Black Cat" is a study of a soul in torment. The source of the torment is what the narrator calls "the spirit of Perverseness." This perverseness, we are told, "is one of the primitive impulses of the human heart-one of the indivisible primary faculties, or sentiments, which give direction to the character of Man." It is this spirit that leads a man to committing a vile act simply because he knows he should not. The narrator further defines this spirit as the "unfathomable longing of the soul to vex itself." Seldom has the impulse been better described that the psychologists call a radical imbalance of personality and the theologians original sin. It is something inherent in the psyche of man.

In advancing such an idea Poe was flying in the face of the Age of Reason. Throughout the eighteenth century both in England and America, the disciples of John Locke taught that the human personality is the sum of all the impressions made upon it from the outside world. Eighteenth century thinkers had carried on a great war to expunge the notion of what they called "innate ideas" from man's thought concerning himself. According to them nothing is innate, all comes from the environment. The ultimate effect of this thinking was destructive of both poetry and religion. It destroyed belief in God and the immortality of the soul. It was the poets more than anyone else who led the attack against Locke in the early nineteenth century, in England Wordsworth and Coleridge, and in America Emerson, Thoreau, and Poe. The romantic poets rediscovered the human soul and Poe made it his chief subject matter. Poe's definition of man's constitutional imbalance of soul is reminiscent of William Faulkner's speech when he received the Nobel Prize. Faulkner, also a southerner, said that the chief subject of the writer was the human heart in contention with itself. In all of Poe no character is more in contention with himself than the narrator of "The Black Cat."

"The Black Cat" was published on August 19, 1843, in the United States Saturday Post, as the Saturday Evening Post was called in those days. The biographical background of the story is more fearful than the tale itself. Poe was afraid of the fits of temper that came over him while he was drinking. When sober he was a gentleman, courteous in any situation, and the very soul of gentility. When he was affected by alcohol, however, the suppressed rage that he felt for what he considered the injustices of a gross and unfeeling world expressed itself in vituperation and violence. In creating the narrator of "The Black Cat" Poe distorted and exaggerated all the faults of his personality while drunk. The narrator is not Poe, but Poe used details of his own experience in the character of the narrator.

ESSAY QUESTIONS AND ANSWERS

Question: What it the effect of the narrator's insistence, at the beginning of the story, that he is not mad?

Answer: When the narrator insists over and over again that he is not mad, the reader is inclined to think just the opposite. In fiction exaggeration often implies the opposite, and Poe was a master of this technique. The reader's conviction of the insanity of the narrator is confirmed by the knowledge that he is to die on the following day, ostensibly for some crime for which he has been condemned. When accosted on the street by a man who tells you again and again that he is not mad, before he even informs you of the reason for his interference with you, you, of course, judge the man to be mad. Poe has arranged the first paragraph so the reader will come to exactly the same conclusion.

Question: Why does Poe have the narrator's house burn down shortly after the killing of the cat?

Answer: There are at least two reasons for Poe to have the narrator's house burn down. He obviously wanted to introduce as a kind of stage prop in the story the gigantic image of the cat on the wall. In order to present the image successfully he contrived to have the house burn down. Secondly, he wants the reader to feel that the narrator is being hounded by a fate that will eventually make him pay for his crimes. Like the Furies of ancient Greek drama, the cat is to pursue the narrator until justice has been done. Having the house burn down directly after the hanging of the cat is an admirable way to suggest that the narrator will be haunted by ill luck until retribution has been done.

THE PREMATURE BURIAL

TEXTUAL ANALYSIS

CHARACTERS

Narrator

PLOT ANALYSIS

The narrator regards burial before death as the most hideous torture that can be endured by man either on earth or in hell. The boundaries between life and death are shadowy and vague. The narrator tells of a number of cases in which people were interred while they were alive, because they appeared to be dead but actually were not. He described in detail the terrors of such a fate: "The unendurable oppression of the lungs-the stifling fumes of the damp earth-the clinging to the death garments-the rigid embrace of the narrow house-the blackness of the absolute Night-the silence like a sea that overwhelms-the unseen but palpable presence of the Conqueror Worm-these things, with the thoughts of the air and grass above, with the memory of dear friends who would fly to save us if but informed of our fate, and with consciousness that of this fate they can never be informed-that our hopeless portion is that of the really dead-these considerations, I say, carry into the heart, which still palpitates, a degree of appalling horror from which the most daring imagination must recoil."

The narrator says that he was subject to attacks of catalepsy in which he appeared to be dead. He became morose and melancholy, lost in reveries of death. In one of his waking dreams he is bidden to arise by a gibbering voice. The voice is that of a fiend who bids him to look around him. He sees all the graves of mankind and in millions of them the corpses struggle to arise. Such dreams or visions drove him to take precautions against his being interred alive. Nevertheless, as he arises from a deep swoon some time later he is afraid to open his eyes because his senses tell him that what he has feared for so long has actually happened. He opens his eyes and sees only dark. Six inches above him he feels solid wood. He smells earth above him. As the conviction that he has been buried alive forces itself into every chamber of his soul he lets out a "long, wild, and continuous shriek." Human voices reply to him and they restore his memory of where he is.

He had accompanied some friends on a gunning expedition on the James River and they had been overtaken by rain. To avoid being soaked they had slept in a small sloop and he had gone to sleep squeezed into a bunk directly under the deck. After his terrifying experience he is cured of his catalepsy and dismisses forever his charnel apprehensions. He becomes a new man. The narrator concludes his account with the reflection that there are demons in the human personality that must sleep or they will devour us. The grim legion of terrors to which the human soul is subject is not altogether fanciful.

CHARACTER ANALYSES

Narrator

The character of the narrator, as is so often the case in Poe, is very much like that of the author. Like Roderick Usher, he is hypersensitive in the extreme to all manner of sense impressions. His mind knows no rest, but is constantly exploring imaginative possibilities. The slightest suggestion will immediately set into action a pattern of thought and imagination, so that he cannot be at rest. His mind leaps from one thing to another with appalling swiftness. He is attracted by the morbid and seems to take a kind of pleasure in imagining himself suffering the terrors of the grave. He is constitutionally pessimistic, always expecting the worst to happen, so much so that the vaguest suggestion that his fears are about to come true will make him react as though all he had feared was indeed coming to pass. He is something of a scholar and his hypochondria drives him to ferret out many cases of premature burial because he is sure this is the fate he will one day suffer.

Comment

In its structure "The Premature Burial" resembles Poe's detective stories. The tale is divided into two parts. The first half of the story consists of a discourse by the narrator in which he describes himself and his ailment and cites several dramatic cases of premature burial. The second half of the story contains all the action. The cases he cites are, in their relationship to the rest of the tale, like the formal statements of the witnesses in the detective stories. They provide the factual foundation for the rest of the story. The ultimate effect and meaning of the piece would be incomplete without them.

"The Premature Burial" is only on the surface a tale of horror whose chief intent is to frighten. It is in its full meaning a tale that gives us a glimpse into the human soul. The chief fact of the narrator's life prior to his frightening experience on the ship is fear. His entire life is dominated by fear. He is afraid of death and yet his morbid imagination is attracted at the same time that it is repelled by all the terrors that tradition assigns to the charnel house. The idea of physical dissolution and confinement in the earth is an obsession with him and it keeps him from living a normal life.

The effect of his experience in the bunk under the deck is to purge the fear from his soul. "I became a new man and lived a man's life. From that memorable night, I dismissed forever my charnel apprehensions, and with them vanished the cataleptic disorder, of which, perhaps, they had been less the consequence than the cause." No other story of Poe's so tempts a psychological interpretation. In particular it fits Freud's idea of psychoanalysis. The victim of neurotic apprehensions, the sufferer from anxiety, actually experiences what he has feared for so long, but in a way that forbids, of course, the ultimate effects of the experience. When he realizes that his fears are illusory he is cured of his illness and begins to lead a healthy life. In one important respect, however, the story does not fit the Freudian pattern. According to Freud we must continually look at the demons of the subconscious so that we may become reconciled to their presence and not let them disturb us in the future. The narrator, however, tells us quite specifically that "they must be suffered to slumber or we perish."

We do not have to refer to Freud, however, in order to understand the insights of the tale into the human soul. The great religions of the world have from time immemorial known that man is subject to demons of the spirit that must be met and conquered if he is to enjoy what is truly life. Again Poe reminds us of the infinite world of spirit that constantly impinges on our lives. His characters are, in a strange way, religious, in the sense that they struggle toward eternal life, the life of the spirit. But their attempts are often based upon false premises, and when they attempt by spurious means, by what is essentially magic rather than virtue, to enter the other world, they are rebuffed and bitterly disappointed

ESSAY QUESTION AND ANSWER

Question: At the beginning of the tale the narrator cites several instances of people being buried while still alive. How are these cases related to the suspense and drama of the story's conclusion?

Answer: Like the factual beginning of "MS. Found in a Bottle," the case histories that the narrator cites cause the reader to give his assent to what appears the truth of the tale. The story begins deceptively like an essay. The tone of the narrator's description of himself and the case histories is detached and objective, almost scientific. The reader believes what he says implicitly, as if he were reading a diary or a journal. When the narrator begins to describe the ghastly experience he has undergone in the ship, for all the reader knows he has actually been buried alive. Poe, of course, does not drop any hints beforehand that the narrator is in a ship. He was too expert a writer to ruin the suspense of the tale in that fashion. As the reader is confronted with the narrator's experience he has in his mind the memory of all the case histories. The narrator has proven premature burial to be not simply possible, but even common, given certain circumstances. Confronted with the fact of the darkness and the wood above the narrator's head, the reader believes along with the narrator that the narrator has been interred while still alive. The case histories are the foundation for the suspense of the conclusion, for without them the reader would be inclined to disbelieve what is happening, or what the narrator thinks is happening.

THE PURLOINED LETTER

TEXTUAL ANALYSIS

CHARACTERS

Narrator

Dupin

Prefect Of Police

PLOT ANALYSIS

On a gusty autumn evening the narrator is enjoying "the twofold luxury of meditation and a meerschaum" with his friend Dupin. They are interrupted by the arrival of the Prefect of Police. He is provided with a pipe and a chair and proceeds to describe a case that is troubling him. He says the affair is both simple and odd, to which Dupin replies that it may be the very simplicity of the matter that disturbs him. The Prefect laughs at what he considers Dupin's folly and begins his story. A letter has been stolen from a woman of social prominence who is associated with men of power in the French government. The letter reveals that she has been having an affair with one of her husband's associates. The Minister D, who took it, has been using the letter to exert political pressure. He knows that the woman involved is aware of his theft. The Minister D is described as a man who dares all things. The problem that the Prefect is faced with is how to acquire the letter. A substantial reward has been offered and the Prefect suggests that he share it with Dupin if the latter is successful in retrieving the letter.

The Prefect says that he has had the apartment of the Minister D searched while he was out. The furniture has been examined for hollow legs and arms and the walls have been examined for secret compartments. Even the grounds and the cellars have been searched, but without success. After describing the external appearance of the letter in detail, the Prefect takes his leave.

When the Prefect next appears in Dupin's library, Dupin gives him the letter but only after the Prefect has written him a check for fifty thousand francs. Dupin explains how in two brief visits with the Minister present he was able to both discover and retrieve the letter that in a week's search the Prefect was unable to uncover. He says that he had decided beforehand that the letter had not been hidden in a secret drawer or anything of the like. The Minister is known to be both a mathematician and a poet. Dupin surmised that such a man would reason that the letter would be more likely to be overlooked if it were simply lying about with some other papers. Dupin called on the Minister and during his visit he noticed a soiled and crumpled letter stuffed in a card-rack. The Minister is known to be both methodical and clean. These facts suggested to Dupin that the Minister had gone out of his way to make this particular letter seem as if it were not important to him. Dupin left, forgetting his snuff box on purpose. The next day he calls for his snuff box and brings with him a facsimile of the letter in question. He had arranged beforehand for a loud disturbance in the street directly under the Minister's window. When the disturbance took place the Minister went to the window. In those few seconds Dupin took the much sought letter from the card-rack and put the facsimile in its place. Dupin takes a particular pleasure in outwitting the Minister as the latter once did him an evil turn.

CHARACTER ANALYSES

Narrator

Since Dupin is provided with all the facts he requires for the solution of the case through the Prefect's narrative, there is no valid work for the narrator who is only present as an observer at the two meetings of the Prefect and Dupin. Dupin, of course, would never entrust to anyone but himself the extremely delicate business of interviewing the Minister.

Dupin

In "The Purloined Letter" Dupin emerges as a character completely in control of both the personal and the intellectual situation. He handles the Prefect with the attitude of a man handling a child. Content in the knowledge that he is the master to whom the outside world must come, Dupin asks the questions and suggests answers. He mystifies the Prefect on purpose by telling him at the very beginning of the tale that it may be the very simplicity of the situation that makes it difficult. We have learned to expect such a comment from Dupin, as in the two other stories in which he appears he elaborates a theory of the importance of the seemingly irrelevant, and has trained his mind to catch the importance of small details. He tells the narrator that the secret of his success is neither luck nor profound analysis, but the ability to identify with his opponent's intellect so that he can correctly reconstruct the course of action involved in the crime.

The Prefect of Police

In "The Murders in the Rue Morgue" and "The Mystery of Marie Roget" the Prefect is not seen in depth. In "The Purloined Letter" Poe gives him true character for the first time. The narrator claims that the Prefect calls "odd" everything that he does not understand, and hence lives amidst many oddities. Throughout this tale the Prefect is seen as a simple though unctuous man with whom Dupin and the narrator have good sport. When Dupin tells him it is the simplicity of the case that has troubled him, he laughs and says: "Dupin, you will be the death of me yet." The Prefect tells us that he does not take the Minister G to be a complete fool, but that since he is a poet he is only one remove from a fool. When the reader comes to this statement he judges the Prefect himself a fool, which is exactly what Poe wants. When Dupin unexpectedly hands the Prefect the letter that has caused him so much trouble, he grasps it in "a perfect agony of joy" and rushes from the room without saying a word. He is a man whose reactions are always immediate and on the surface.

Comment

"The Purloined Letter" is one of Poe's most successful tales. It is certainly the most tightly constructed of his detective stories. Poe wrote at length on what he considered the proper method of constructing short fiction. His theories demand a tale in which nothing is superfluous. Everything must contribute directly to the unfolding of the plot or it should be dispensed with. Many critics feel that his detective stories violate his own ideas of how a story should be constructed because the action ends before the story in all three cases. That is, the action itself concludes and Dupin's explanation is allowed to end the story. However, what must be taken into consideration is that these are detective stories. The rational explanation of method is an intrinsic part of such a story and certainly the story would seem odd without it. It is true that Poe's explanations of method tend to come all in one section at the end of the tale, but they then appear in the nature of afterthoughts on the action which Dupin shares with the narrator. There is an atmosphere of a storm weathered as in the cozy library Dupin explains, step by step, his method of analysis. The fact that these stories have always been considered three of Poe's best is ample evidence that his method is successful, whatever objections may be brought against it in theory.

The dialogue in the tale is worthy of note for its economy, its sense of drama, and restrained urgency. It is reminiscent of the magnificent, clipped dialogue of "The Cask of Amontillado." The following sequence of lines is a good example.

"What nonsense you do talk!" replied the Prefect, laughing heartily. "Perhaps the mystery is a little too plain," said Dupin. "Oh good heavens! who ever heard of such an idea?" "A little to self evident." "Ha! ha! ha! - ha! ha! ha! - ho! ho! ho!" roared our visitor, profoundly amused, "Oh, Dupin, you will be the death of me yet!"

We have here not the self-consciously mannered dialogue of a Henry James, but rather a dialogue produced by an extremely energetic imagination that has thrust itself wholeheartedly into the literary undertaking at hand and is obviously enjoying it immensely. Poe's intense imagination and his capacity to lose himself in a fictional world are unequaled. The result is a tale that is gripping both emotionally and intellectually.

ESSAY QUESTIONS AND ANSWERS

Question: In all three of his detective stories Poe elaborates the idea that the imagination of the poet as well as the analytical ability of the scientist is needed to solve mysteries successfully. How is this idea built into the framework of "The Purloined Letter"?

Answer: The Minister G is both a poet and a mathematician, and therefore he is Dupin's most formidable opponent. The Prefect is no match for him because the Prefect scorns the poetic imagination. He can think only of his own ideas, and cannot fathom the working of a mind so much more sophisticated than his own. Dupin says that had the Minister been only a mathematician he would have been at the mercy of the Prefect whose methods are mechanical and carried out with mechanical perfection. Abstract intelligence often fails when applied to human situations. Therefore, the man who will solve the mysteries of crime most readily will be the man who has insight into personality as well as logic and science. The Minister was able to see at once what the Prefect would do, and disposed of the letter in a way that would confound him. He was able to perform that act of imaginative identification with his foe that Dupin says is necessary for success. He is successful with the Prefect in the same way that Dupin is successful with him. It was an axiom of Poe's day that intuitive truth was ultimately superior to the truth of pure analytical reason, and he built that concept in many of his tales.

Question: How does Poe use his knowledge of language, literature, and little known titles and names to impress the reader with Dupin's knowledge?

    Answer: Throughout the tale Poe has Dupin use Latin phrases and quotations. The knowledge of Latin was considered in Poe's day the mark of an erudite man, and to a certain degree this still remains true. Poe has Dupin use Latin to impress the reader with his erudition. He makes reference to such things as the differential calculus with the air of one who knows all. At the end of the tale he refers to Crebillon's Atree. Poe, then, through literary **allusion** and reference to mathematical and linguistic matters, impresses the reader with the breadth of Dupin's intellect.

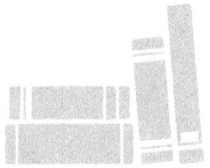

THE FACTS IN THE CASE OF M. VALDEMAR

TEXTUAL ANALYSIS

CHARACTERS

Narrator

PLOT ANALYSIS

The narrator states that he will now present the facts in the astonishing case of M. Valdemar. It had occurred to the narrator that no one had ever been mesmerized in the moment of dying. He was fascinated by the idea that the encroachments of death might be arrested by hypnosis. He arranged to perform the experiment with one M. Valdemar who was then dying of an advanced phthisis. He received a note from the gentleman himself stating that his doctors agree he is close to death and that the experiment must be performed immediately. When he arrives he finds the subject in an advanced state of emaciation, so much so that the cheek bones had broken through the skin. He was obviously in the death agony and the narrator proceeded to mesmerize him. To questions asked him after he had been put into the trance Valdemar replied that he felt no pain, that he was asleep and dying. Shortly after speaking his jaw fell open, revealing a blackened tongue. The observers concluded that he had died and consigned him to the nurses, but at that moment, from the motionless jaws came a voice: "Yes;-no;-I have been sleeping-and now-now I am dead." The voice seems to come from a great distance and frightens them all horribly. They attempt to draw blood from Valdemar's arm, but are unable to do so. Valdemar remained in this state for exactly seven months. At the end of the seven months it was decided to try the experiment of waking him from the hypnotic trance. As the narrator-hypnotist addressed the subject his tongue began to quiver. The same horrible voice that spoke to them before speaks again: "For God's sake! - quick! - quick! - put me to sleep - or, quick! - waken me! - quick! - I say to you that I am dead!" As the narrator made the proper mesmeric passes with his hands and the subject began to waken, the body rotted away before their eyes. "Upon the bed, before that whole company, there lay a nearly liquid mass of loathsome-of detestable putrescence."

CHARACTER ANALYSIS

Narrator

In the narrator of this tale we see yet another side of Poe's varied personality. The narrator is a scientist. He is animated and driven by curiosity. His attitude is detached and objective. We learn nothing about his personality or that of M. Valdemar. His account of what happens reads like a lab report. It is filled with exact references to time and the condition of the subject. The only time that the narrator registers emotion is when Valdermar speaks, and then he states simply that all the observers were horrified. Throughout his life Poe maintained a very great interest in science. As a young man he was an amateur naturalist and collected shells. He read widely in standard scientific works of the day. Throughout his editorial career he reviewed books of science as well as books in the general area of the humanities. He expressed some of his interest in science in the detective stories, but the narrator of "The Facts in the Case of M. Valdemar" is more purely a scientist than Dupin.

Comment

Hypnotism and magnetism were matters of scientific speculation that fascinated the general public in the mid-nineteenth century in much the same way that space travel fascinates us. The exact nature of these phenomena had not been established, and the uncertainty lent itself readily to the literary imagination. Poe's tales dealing with hypnotism can be considered early science fiction stories. Along with Jules Vernes, Poe was one of the writers who helped to establish science fiction as a minor category of modern literature. It demonstrates the extent to which his imagination was quick to seize upon materials currently of interest to the general public and incorporate them in fiction.

"The Facts in the Case of M. Valdemar" was published in the American Review for December 1845. Its success was immediate. Elizabeth Barrett was horrified by the tale. In London the story was published as a true account under the title "Mesmerism in Articulo Mortis." A gentleman from Scotland wrote to Poe and asked whether or not the story were true. In France the compiler of the Dictionnaire des Superstitions Populaires referred to the case of M. Valdemar as a true one. The number of people who took the story to be a true account indicates that one reason for its success was its realism. Poe's reportorial style seemed so much like the language of an actual account that it demanded belief.

ESSAY QUESTION AND ANSWER

Question: Discuss Poe's use of technical scientific language in "The Facts in the Case of M. Valdemar."

Answer: In Valdemar, Poe has the narrator use technical language that lends an atmosphere of **realism** and immediacy to the tale. He refers to Valdemar's disease as "a confirmed phthisis." In describing the subject's physical condition Poe wrote: "The left lung had been for eighteen months in a semi-osseous or cartilaginous state, and was, of course, entirely useless for all purposes of vitality." The phrase "purulent tuburcles" is used in describing the right lung. They suspect the subject is suffering from "aneurism of the aorta." It is typical of Poe to use a technical vocabulary early in the tale to convince the reader of the truth of the narrative. He used this technique in "MS. Found in a Bottle." The events that would be more likely to inspire disbelief are kept for the latter part of the tale so the reader will not encounter them until he has already given imaginative assent to the story.

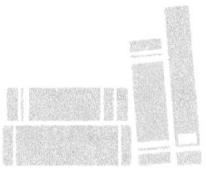

THE CASK OF AMONTILLADO

TEXTUAL ANALYSIS

CHARACTERS

Montresor

Fortunato

PLOT ANALYSIS

Montresor has been insulted by Fortunato and vows revenge. He decides that his revenge will be both slow and sweet, and that in order to enjoy his revenge completely Fortunato must know that he, Montresor, is taking revenge upon him. Montresor knows that Fortunato is a connoisseur of wine, and evolves a plan that will take advantage of his enemy's chief characteristic. "During the supreme madness of the carnival season" he tells Fortunato that he has acquired a pipe of wine that passes for amontillado. He wants Fortunato to accompany him to his wine cellar and test the wine for him.

Fortunato agrees to the plan and goes with Montresor to his palazzo. Each bearing torches, they descend into the catacombs of the Montresors. Fortunato has a cough and is unsteady on his feet. After a fit of coughing Montresor knocks the head from a bottle of Medoc and offers Fortunato a drink. Fortunato drinks to Montresor's buried ancestors and Montresor drinks to long life.

The ceiling and walls of the vault are covered with niter. They descend farther until they are under the river bed and the niter hangs like moss all about them. Again Fortunato has a fit of coughing and again Montresor gives him a bottle of wine, this time De Grave. By this time Fortunato is feeling the effect of the wine, but is no less eager to taste the amontillado. They pass under a row of low arches and arrive at a deep crypt. Its walls are lined with human remains. At the rear of the crypt is a small recess. Montresor tells him the amontillado is just ahead. Fortunato, however, collides with a wall of solid rock. He stands bewildered as Montresor fetters him to two iron staples in the granite. Montresor then uncovers some building stone and mortar and begins to wall Fortunato in the crypt. As the rows of masonry grow higher and higher Fortunato begins to moan. He has recovered from his drunkenness and realizes what is happening to him. He begins to scream maniacally and says that the joke is over. Montresor says that it is indeed time to go and prepares to lay the last tier of masonry. He plasters in the last stone and piles against the wall a rampart of bones, leaving Fortunato to a slow death in the crypt.

CHARACTER ANALYSES

Fortunato

Fortunato is an eminently successful man. He enjoys the good things of life, is clever and has no scruples. Montresor tells us that, regarding paintings and gems he is a complete quack, but uses what small knowledge he has "to practice imposture upon the British and American millionaires." Only in the matter of old wines is he sincere, and he prides himself upon his connoisseurship. His delight in the nuances of appreciating wine is the only artistic feature of a rather plodding character. He is not, in general, a man of taste or feeling, and has little regard for anything but the immediate facts of material existence.

Montresor

Like Poe, Montresor is a man of spirit. He cannot abide the condescending attitude and insults of Fortunato. Fortunato's grossness and failure to appreciate the finer things in life drive him to a frenzy. When he decides to revenge himself he lingers over it, enjoying every moment. He plots revenge as though he were creating a great work of art. The story is told through the words of Montresor, and his consciousness dominates the tale. This is peculiarly fitting, since Montresor's mind is one that delights in communicating moments of glory.

Comment

"The Cask of Amontillado" was written in 1846. It is a story of revenge, and reflects Poe's intense desire to punish a number of people who had been making trouble for him. He had written a glowing review of the poetry of one Mrs. Osgood for the March issue of Godey's, and she had written him a number of effusive letters, one of which attracted the attention of a Mrs. Elizabeth Ellet, herself a poetess. Gossip ran freely, and a delegation, including Margaret Fuller, a famous woman intellectual of the day, called on Poe to claim the letters. Poe, however, sent them to Mrs. Ellet's house instead. Mrs. Ellet's brother-in-law began to threaten Poe. Before the affair had settled down Poe was involved in a fistfight. An article attacking him was published on May 26 in the Mirror. Poe was not one to give up easily once he had been aroused. The winning of over $200 in a law suit placated him, however, and he worked out the rest of his ire in "The Cask of Amontillado." In Poe's mind his life had once again been made difficult by a gross and unfeeling world. Such a feeling lies behind his characterization of Fortunato. He projected in Fortunato all that he detested in a world of Philistines.

The tale is the most tightly knit of any he ever wrote. The opening sentence proclaims Montresor's desire for revenge and from that point onward the story proceeds inevitably to the act of vengeance. In its effortless unfolding from detail to detail, the story is reminiscent of "The Gold Bug" and the three detective stories involving Dupin. "The Cask of Amontillado" is a more balanced tale than those, however, because it contains far more dialogue. The dialogue is clipped and concise, as befits the tenseness of the situation. The last words between Fortunato and Montresor constitute the finest passage of its kind in all Poe. Fortunato has been watching the wall grow higher and higher. At last he speaks, in a voice Montresor can hardly recognize, so changed has it been by grisly fear.

"But is it not getting late? Will not they be awaiting us at the palazzo, the Lady Fortunato and the rest? Let us be gone." "Yes,"

I said, "let us be gone." "For the love of God, Montresor!" "Yes," I said "for the love of God!"

What could be more utterly frustrating and horrible to Fortunato than the monotonous repetition of his own request by a man who has no intention of granting it? And when he makes his final, almost inarticulate plea, this also is repeated. Fortunato does not speak again. The implication is that his mind snaps. We have already been told that his screams are hysterical and mindless. Twice Montresor speaks to him after his last fearful ejaculation, but no words are spoken from behind the barrier, which is then sealed forever.

ESSAY QUESTIONS AND ANSWERS

Question: Discuss Poe's use of humor in "The Cask of Amontillado."

Answer: Poe's humor in "The Cask of Amontillado" is characterized by **irony**. Irony is a conscious simulation of ignorance for purposes of humor and **satire**. An ironical expression is one that implies the opposite of what it states. When Montresor first lashes Fortunato to the wall, he toys with him by speaking as though the latter could leave at his own free will.

"Pass your hand," I said, "over the wall; you cannot help feeling the niter. Indeed, it is very damp. Once more let me implore you to return. No? Then I must positively leave you. But first I must render you all the little attentions in my power."

Fortunato cannot leave, and therefore Montresor's statement becomes ironic as well as humorous. The "little attentions"

Montresor is going to render to Fortunato are not, we know, attentions at all. Again he means the opposite of what he says, to what extent becomes obvious when he begins to lay the tiers of masonry. Again, at the very conclusion of the tale, when Montresor mindlessly repeats Fortunato's frantic requests, the statements are ironic. Montresor's dialogue is amusing because it is clever and ironic. The humor of the tale, however, is not the open, sunny humor of a Mark Twain. It is rather the humor of a mind twisted by desire for revenge.

Question: Discuss the means by which Montresor coaxes Fortunato into the catacombs.

Answer: Montresor knows that Fortunato's head can be turned by flattery. He plots Fortunato's downfall as shrewdly as Dupin solves mysteries. He appeals to Fortunato's sense of his own importance by consulting him in the first place. Before Fortunato can reply, Montresor says that he is on his way to Luchesi, since Fortunato is obviously engaged in the festivities of the hour. Fortunato immediately falls into the trap by saying that Luchesi is no judge of wine and that he will go himself. The victim has swallowed the bait.

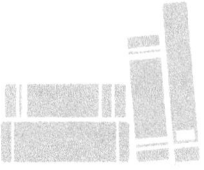

ULALUME

TEXTUAL ANALYSIS

FORM

"Ulalume" is a stanzaic poem. There are nine stanzas in the poem, each consisting of ten lines. The **rhyme** scheme is A - B - B - A - B - A - B - A - B. The meter of the poem is iambic **trimeter**, that is, the first syllable is unaccented and there are three accents or beats in every line. The anapestic foot is often substituted for the iambic.

SUMMARY

In ashen-skied October the poet travels with his Soul to "the dank tarn of Auber/In the ghoul-haunted woodland of Weir." He says he had been there once before. His heart is like restless lava. He and his Soul distrust both the place and their memory of it. As dawn approaches a crescent moon appears, the moon of Astarte. Psyche, the Soul, distrusts the moon of Astarte and begs the poet to hasten. They come to the end of a vista and stop by the door of a "legended tomb." The Soul tells the poet it is the tomb of his lost Ulalume. The poet recalls that exactly a year ago he had buried his lover in this tomb. The poem ends with a rhetorical question. The poet asks what demon has tempted him to this frightening place at such a time.

Comment

"Ulalume" is a poem dealing with two different kinds of love, physical and spiritual. The poet is suffering temptations of a sensual nature. We are told his heart is volcanic, which suggests both the heat and unrest of passion. When the crescent moon of Astarte first comes out the poet is immediately attracted to it. Astarte was an ancient Near Eastern goddess of fertility. The crescent moon, then, is a symbol of sensual passion. The poet's Soul, however, immediately insists on leaving the place, realizing the danger, and they pass on. She requires the poet to be true to his lost Ulalume who is his true, his spiritual love. The poet may well ask what demon had tempted him to travel to the tomb of his beloved, for the trip had indeed been filled with temptations. His Soul has saved him, however, by being instantly aware of the danger.

The descriptive background of "Ulalume" is reminiscent of "The Fall of the House of Usher." In both the poem and the story there is a misty land, a swamp. In both the atmosphere is colorless, gray, ashen, suggesting dissolution and decay. The descent of the poet takes place in October, and the time of year in the story is autumn. The descent in the poem is a descent into the poet's unconscious as well as a descent into his past. He is drawn by both physical and spiritual love, the two possibilities of his consciousness which he must face in order to decide between them.

ESSAY QUESTION AND ANSWER

Question: Discuss the poem as a little drama.

Answer: The basic situation of the poem is dramatic because it involves temptation and choice. The poet is torn between the decision of his Soul and the temptation of Astarte, or his purely sensual unconscious. The poem is a drama of self in a moment of crisis. The poet is first tempted by his sensual unconscious. His heart is tumultuous and responds to the temptation of Astarte. In the moment of crisis, however, his Soul keeps him from destruction by insisting that they leave. The discovery of the tomb reminds the poet of his lost lover to whom he must be true. She represents spiritual love to which the poet is faithful in the poem.

ELDORADO

TEXTUAL ANALYSIS

FORM

"Eldorado" is a stanzaic poem. Each stanza consists of six lines. The **rhyme** scheme is A - A - B -C - C - B. The first two lines and the third and fourth lines of each **stanza** are written in iambic **dimeter**, while the third and sixth lines are in iambic **trimeter**. The poet has not altered the form in any of the stanzas.

SUMMARY

A gaily clad knight had journeyed in search of Eldorado. He grew old in his quest. As his strength failed him he met a pilgrim and asked the way to Eldorado. The pilgrim tells him he must ride over the Mountains of the Moon and through the Valley of the Shadow if he wishes to find Eldorado.

Comment

"Eldorado" is a perfectly realized lyric poem and one of Poe's masterpieces. The form of the poem is original and its short, staccato lines perfectly suit the **theme** of a search on horseback. The action of the poem is simple and direct. The **theme** of the poem is based upon the legend of a fabulous country or city which was believed by the Spaniards and Sir Walter Raleigh to exist on the banks of the Amazon or Orinoco. It was supposed to abound in gold, and the name means "the gilded one." The idea of the city of gold has often been used by writers, including Voltaire in his Candide.

ESSAY QUESTION AND ANSWER

Question: What does Eldorado stand for in the poem?

Answer: The meaning of Eldorado in the poem is left indefinite on purpose. We are only told that the knight in searching for Eldorado; we do not know why he wants to get there. However, precisely because of the indefinite nature of the knight's quest, Eldorado comes to stand for the fulfillment of the heart's desire. It is that land where the troubled lose their troubles and where suffering will cease. It becomes, in short, an analogue for heaven. The pilgrim says the knight must ride through the Valley of the Shadow, which strengthens its association with heaven. The knight's quest becomes the quest of all of us for perfect peace. The **theme** of the poem is universal. Like all great art it transcends the purely personal experience and reaches out to all men.

THE BELLS

TEXTUAL ANALYSIS

FORM

"The Bells" is cast in the form of an irregular ode. Greek odes were highly formal pieces reserved for the most august **themes** and occasions. In the Renaissance a number of English poets, including Ben Jonson and Cowley, began to write irregular odes. An irregular ode is an ode that is not arranged in sections of the same elaborate form. The separate sections may suggest a similar form, but upon analysis one finds that the poet has simply allowed the poem to evolve around a number of core lines, concepts and verbal parallels, without attempting to force the poem into a form that is the same in all its sections. There are four sections in "The Bells," of 14, 21, 34 and 44 lines respectively.

SUMMARY

The entire poem is an injunction to the reader to listen to the bells, the different varieties of which the poet then attempts to evoke in all their multitude of effects. We are told to listen to wedding bells, alarm bells, silver bells, and iron bells. In the first section Poe writes of the silver bells: "What a world of merriment their melody foretells!" In each of the four sections there are similar lines and the repetition of them helps to tie the poem together. In the second section he writes of the wedding bells: "What a world of happiness their harmony foretells!" In the third section he writes of the alarm bells: "What a tale of terror, now, their turbulency tells!" In the fourth section he writes of the iron bells: "What a world of solemn thought their melody compels." The word bells is frequently repeated in the poem, sometimes four or five times in a single line.

Comment

"The Bells" is a poem whose only reason for existence is sound. It is an experiment in which Poe sought to exploit to the fullest the resources of the English language for producing musical effects. Many of the lines are constructed around alliterating words, the chief intention of which is to produce verbal melody. For example, in the first section he wrote: "What a world of merriment their melody foretells!" The repeated w's and m's are balanced nicely by the l's at the end of foretells which suggest the hard ring of bells. The chief devices used in the poem are **alliteration**, repetition, and **rhyme**. The poem is not at all typical of Poe, but is rather an experiment, and as such it cannot really be compared with the rest of his work.

ESSAY QUESTION AND ANSWER

Question: Even into such a poem as "The Bells" Poe manages to introduce his favorite **theme** of the supernatural. Discuss this theme in the poem.

Answer: In describing the iron bells in the fourth section of the poem, Poe tells us their tone is menacing. His imagination then postulates ghouls living alone in the bell tower. They take joy in the melancholy monotone of their bells that is like a stone rolled upon the human heart. Even in an experimental poem Poe could not resist interjecting the **theme** of the supernatural.

ANNABEL LEE

TEXTUAL ANALYSIS

FORM

"Annabel Lee" is a lyric poem of six stanzas. The stanzas consist of 6, 6, 8, 6, 7, and 8 lines respectively. The stanzas, then, follow no general rule, although they stay closest to the pattern of the first, second, and fourth stanzas. The poem is written in lines alternating between iambic **tetrameter**, or lines of four accents beginning with an unaccented syllable, and iambic **trimeter**, or lines of three accents beginning with an unaccented syllable. In the fifth **stanza** the second and third lines are both **trimeter** and do not alternate. In the last **stanza** the fifth and sixth lines are both **tetrameter** and do not alternate.

SUMMARY

> The poet says that many years ago in a kingdom by the sea he was in love with the girl whose name is the title of the poem. They were both children and she had no other thought than to love and be loved by the poet. Even the angelic hosts of heaven are jealous of their love. The girl, however, dies and is shut up in a sepulcher by her "high-born kinsman." Their

> love is stronger than death, and the poet says their souls can never be parted. Every night he lies down by her side in the sepulcher by the sea.

Comment

"Annabel Lee" is a romantic lyric. The point of the poem is not so much to tell a story as it is to evoke a mood, to suggest a feeling, to make the reader feel what the poet feels. The feeling the poet deals with is the loss of love, which is treated from the point of view of romantic nostalgia. One cannot expect from such a poem a completely logical development, and there are details of the poem that defy common sense and for which no explanation is given.

The love the poem celebrates is the very quintessence of romantic love. It is a love that is more than love. Such exaggeration is an essential part of the poem. They are children, but they are far wiser than many older than they. In its celebration of the love of children the poem is reminiscent of Wordsworth's "Immortality Ode" in which the consciousness of the child is exalted over that of the adult. After she dies his life becomes meaningless. He dreams of her and lies down by her body in the sepulcher. Though separated in body they are united in spirit. The poem glorifies romantic love that survives death.

ESSAY QUESTION AND ANSWER

Question: In two places Poe changes the alternating pattern of **tetrameter** and **trimeter** lines. Why does he change the pattern in these two places?

Answer: One way for a poet to achieve a special emphasis is by altering a pattern with which the reader has become familiar and which he has learned to expect. In the fifth **stanza** both the second and third lines are **trimeter**: "Of those who were older than we - Of many far wiser than we-." The effect of the change in the pattern in this particular case is to emphasize the idea that the love of the young couple is something special, indeed. In the fifth and sixth lines of the last **stanza** the meter is **tetrameter**: "And so, all the night-tide, I lie down by the side/ Of my darling-my darling-my life and my bride." In this case the breaking of the formal pattern emphasizes the closeness of the lovers in spite of their separation, a paradox that is often at the heart of the tradition of romantic love.

CONCLUSION

POE AS EDITOR

Poe was the first really modern editor in American periodical literature. He took his job seriously. Before he began to work for the *Southern Literary Messenger*, that magazine and others like it had been directed chiefly toward a female audience that required, it was thought, sentimental fiction and poetry, anything but serious writing. Under Poe's tutelage American periodicals began to accept and encourage really professional work. When Poe reviewed a book he would tear it to pieces if he thought it was hack work. No one before him had been so uncompromisingly honest as an editor. He dispelled the clouds of romance and put the management of literary periodicals upon the basis of actual merit.

POE AS LITERARY CRITIC

As a literary critic Poe was ahead of his time. He was never content to brush off a book with pleasant generalities, but held both the writer and himself to a close analysis of the text, utilizing frequent quotation and line-by-line commentary. He foreshadowed the so-called "New Critics," who in the twentieth century insisted upon looking at the individual work of art as a self-contained unit with laws of its own. He was tirelessly detailed in his reviews, always documenting his opinions with a multitude of concrete examples. He was, in short, the father of modern American literary criticism.

POE'S INFLUENCE

Poe's impact on French literature was immediate. Mallarme translated "The Raven" and followed it with a translation of Poe's poems in rhythmic prose. Baudelaire wrote the first European biography of Poe. He took Poe as his literary model, and Poe's influence is obvious in The Flowers of Evil. In the latter part of the century Poe's influence passed over to England to inspire Aubrey Beardsley and Oscar Wilde. Swinburne and Rossetti already knew his work. In Italy Poe's influence was seen in the characterization in D' Annunzio's novels and plays. Dostoevski's tortured and self-questioning characters owe much to Poe.

For the first time in American literary history an American writer had significantly influenced literary Europe. Poe's blending of love and death, of yearning intensified by the certainty of loss, flowed through the stream of European literature. The neurotic, aesthetic hero came into his own and enjoyed repeated incarnations.

POE AND IMAGISM

Poe's technique in poetry was much imitated in the late nineteenth century. His use of symbols and images to suggest rather than state the complex of ideas and emotions that he wanted to communicate is far closer to modern poetry than to the poets that immediately followed him. His influence can be seen in the movement known as **imagism** which flowered in England in the early twentieth century and which emphasized the purely pictorial in poetry.

HIS REPUTATION

In France Poe has always been considered a great lyric poet. In Europe, in general, he is accepted as a writer of major importance. In this country he is largely unappreciated by modern writers in the north who often consider him a hack. Taken up with immediate social problems, they cannot see in Poe's weird stories anything that can speak to the present generation. His reputation in the north still suffers from the rumors that circulated shortly after his death that associated him with drugs and insanity. Despite all the biographies of Poe that have been written we still lack a major and balanced work by a first-rate scholar. A new edition of Poe's complete works, which is now in preparation, should do much toward providing us with a more accurate picture of Poe as one of the classic American writers.

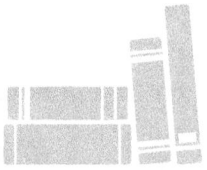

BIBLIOGRAPHY

PRIMARY SOURCES

The Complete Works of Edgar Allan Poe, ed. James A. Harrison. 17 vols. New York, 1902.

The Poems of Edgar Allan Poe, ed. Killis Campbell. Boston, 1917.

The Letters of Edgar Allan Poe, ed. John Ward Ostrom. Cambridge, Mass., 1948.

SECONDARY SOURCES

General Background

Literary History of the United States, ed. Spiller, Thorpe, Canby, Johnson. 3 vols. New York, 1946.

Parrington, Vernon Louis, "Edgar Allan Poe." *The Romantic Revolution in America, 1800 - 1860*. New York, 1927.

Books

Allen, Hervey. *Israfel: The Life and Times of Edgar Allan Poe.* 2 vols. New York, 1926.

Bittner, William. *Poe: A Biography.* Boston, 1962.

Cabiaire, Celestin P. *The Influence of Edgar Allan Poe in France.* New York, 1927.

Campbell, Killis. *The Mind of Poe and Other Studies.* Cambridge, 1933.

Canby, Henry Seidel. "Edgar Allan Poe," *Classic Americans.* New York, 1931.

Davidson, Edward H. *Poe: A Critical Study.* Cambridge, Mass., 1957.

Fagin, N. Bryllion. *The Histrionic Mr. Poe.* Baltimore, 1949.

Jackson, David K. *Poe and the Southern Literary Messenger.* Richmond, 1934.

Krutch, Joseph W. *Edgar Allan Poe: A Study in Genius.* New York, 1926.

Moss, Sidney. *Poe's Literary Battles.* Durham, N. C., 1963.

Quinn, Arthur H. *Edgar Allan Poe: A Critical Biography.* New York, 1941.

Quinn, Patrick F. *French Face of Edgar Poe.* Carbondale, Illinois, 1957.

Wagenknecht, Edward. *Edgar Allan Poe: The Man Behind the Legend.* New York, 1963.

Winwar, Frances. *The Haunted Palace: A Life of Edgar Allan Poe.* New York, 1959.

Articles

Bailey, J. O., "Sources for Poe's *Arthur Gordon Pym*, 'Hans Pfall,' and Other Pieces," *PMLA*, LVII (June, 1942), 513 - 535.

Baldwin, Summerfield, "The Aesthetic Theory of Edgar Poe," *Sewanee Review*, XXVI (April, 1918), 210 - 221.

Blair, Walter, "Poe's Conception of Incident and Tone in the Tale," *Modern Philology*, XLI (May, 1944), 226 - 240.

Cox, John L., "Poet as Critic," *English Journal*, coll. ed., XXI (November, 1932), 757 - 763.

Gregory, Horace, "Within the Private View: A Note on Rereading the Poetry of Edgar Allan Poe," *Partisan Review* (May - June, 1943).

Lafleur, Laurence S., "Edgar Allan Poe as Philosopher," *Personalist*, XXII (1941), 401 - 405.

Lind, Sidney, "Poe and Mesmerism," *PMLA*, LXII (December, 1947), 1077 - 1093.

More, Paul Elmer, "A Note on Poe's Method," *Studies in Philology*, XX (July, 1923), 302 - 309.

Pruette, Lorine, "A Psycho-Analytic Study of Edgar Allan Poe," *The American Journal of Psychology*, XXXI (October, 1920), 370 - 402.

Stovall, Floyd, "Poe's Debt to Coleridge," *University of Texas Studies in English*, X (1930), 70 -127.

Walcott, Charles Child, "The Logic of Poe," *College English*, II (Feb., 1941), 438 - 444.

Werner, W. L., "Poe's Theories and Practice in Poetic Technique," *American Literature*, II (May, 1930), 157 - 165.

www.ingramcontent.com/pod-product-compliance
Lightning Source LLC
LaVergne TN
LVHW011711060526
838200LV00051B/2860